THE MAGIC WORLD OF ROSES

the magic world of roses

MATTHEW A.R. BASSITY

HEARTHSIDE PRESS INC. • Publishers • New York

Frontispiece. *An unusual study—made by David L. Strout, Director of the Hallmark Gallery, for an exhibit depicting the development of a new rose.*

Dedicated to

MRS. LYNDON B. JOHNSON

whose inspirational leadership has reawakened
a national awareness of the natural beauty that
is a priceless part of our heritage. It is hoped
that this book will contribute in some measure
to the continued success of the national program
to beautify America.

IN APPRECIATION

In the magic world of roses one name stands out above all others—Jackson & Perkins. This firm began growing roses in 1872 at Newark, New York, in a greenhouse constructed of secondhand glass recovered from a renovated church. Today it is by far the world's largest grower of roses and enjoys an enviable reputation based on a long history of major contributions to the flower that ranks first among America's home gardeners. Many individuals in the firm gave the author invaluable assistance, especially Mrs. Herbert H. Lunay whose department supplied a wealth of data. With some exceptions, listed below, all black and white illustrations and color plates were furnished by Jackson & Perkins.

In addition, the author is indebted to O. Keister Evans, Executive Secretary of the American Rose Society; Dr. Paul R. Krone, Executive Director of Roses Incorporated; George E. Rose, Director of Public Relations, All-America Rose Selections; Rudolph C. Kalmbach, Director of the International Test Gardens at Portland, Oregon; *McCall's Magazine* for the use of color plates published in their August, 1966, edition; Hallmark Cards Inc. for illustrations from their exhibition, "The Rose"; Jack McIntyre, President of the Canadian Centennial Rose Foundation, for the Canadian Centennial color plate; Henry B. Aul for his line drawings illustrating ways to use roses; *Popular Gardening Magazine*; and the following photographers: Gottscho & Schleisner; John Staby; Kenneth Durfee; Vincent Lisanti; Dick Marshall; John P. Roche; Don Marvin and Walter Latoski of Eastman Kodak Company; and Paul E. Genereux.

Matthew A. R. Bassity
Ho-Ho-Kus, New Jersey

CONTENTS

shots . . . *mechanical aids and techniques . . . background material . . . needle-point holders, picture frame . . . photo montage . . . water . . . accessories that connote name or quality of a rose . . . how to pose a rose . . . how to light it indoors . . . rose arrangement pictures . . . problems of black and white photography . . . composition.*

1

THE MYSTIQUE
OF THE ROSE

The Rose distills a healing balm
The beating pulse of pain to calm.
ANACREON
563-478 B.C.

Ever since the beginning of written history the rose has represented the epitome of perfection. Countless individuals have succumbed to its spell, yet no one can define precisely what it is that comprises the lure of roses.

Finding a single definition is comparable to searching for the perfect rose. There never will be one because the outline of perfection varies with each pair of eyes. The rose is a highly subjective experience. It inspires, elevates and calms, excites and soothes. Poets, painters and writers as well as plain dirt gardeners have found it absorbing and completely enchanting.

In nature there is no flower more durable than the rose. Paleobotanists have proved that the rose flourished on earth long before man made his appearance about 700,000 years ago. The earliest evidence would place it back in the Eocene Epoch, some sixty million years ago. If ever there was a Garden of Eden it is fair to say that its loveliest flower was the rose.

Down through the years the rose has adapted itself to an amazingly wide range of climates. But one wonders whether the ever-present thorn was not a factor in its survival during the centuries when vast quantities of plant material were required to satisfy the gargantuan appetites of dinosaurs and other outsize vegetarians.

At any rate, it did survive and some forty million years ago a rose left its imprint on a slate deposit at Florissant, Colorado, eloquently buttressing the argument that the rose is as native to America as the eagle, and is a logical choice for our national flower.

Proof that the ubiquitous rose was a familiar flower during the early civilizations of Northern Hemisphere countries rests in the fact that the word *rose* is among the handful of Indo-European root words that are common to many languages. In English, French, Danish and Norwegian its name is *rose;*

in Italian, Spanish, Portuguese and Latin, *rosa;* in Swedish, *ros;* in Dutch, *roos;* in Bohemian, *ruze;* in Hungarian, *rocza;* in Russian, *roja;* in Polish, *roza;* in German, *rosen;* in Greek, *rhoden.*

The agreement among nations about its name helps not at all when we try to describe the multiple facets of the rose's personality. Many attempts, and this book is another, have been made to isolate and define the qualities of the rose that have enraptured king and commoner for as long as man has existed.

One of the earliest writers to describe the rose was the Greek poet, Sappho, who lived six hundred years before Christ. She wrote:

> Would Jove appoint some flower to reign
> In matchless beauty on the plain,
> The Rose (mankind will all agree),
> The Rose the queen of flowers should be.

Rose perfume is the subject of a delightful Indian legend about an ordinary lump of clay which was asked, "What art thou?" It replied: "I am but a lump of clay but I was placed beside a rose and I caught its fragrance."

In one of his essays, the English critic, John Ruskin, wrote: "Perhaps few people have ever asked themselves why they admire the rose so much, more than all other flowers. If they consider, they will find first that red is, in a delicately graduated state, the liveliest of all pure colors, and secondly, there

1. *Paleobotanists at the Smithsonian Institution estimate the age of this rose leaflet, which was found at Florissant, Colorado, to be more than 40 million years old. It is* Rosa hilliae Lesquereux.

is in the rose no shadow except that which is composed of color. All its shadows are fuller in color than its lights, owing to the translucency and reflective powers of its leaves."

Though Ruskin found physical reasons for the popularity of the rose many have likened it to gods or have attributed to it human traits. Perhaps this is the secret of its indefinable lure?

There's something compelling about a rose. Once you have grown your first rose bush your life may not change radically, but don't count on it. One thing is certain, you will never forget the moment when the June buds begin to open and your first flower gradually unfolds into something so exquisite that you want to stop the clock and preserve it forever. Just as it passes its prime another flower reaches its peak, and then another. With each succeeding bloom you wonder how anything can be so perfect. You may even wonder if this perfection is the result of a latent talent that only you possess.

When you finally realize that there are other perfect rose blossoms in neighboring gardens, grown by people no more skilled than you are, then you graduate into the fraternity of rose growers. This group encompasses about as wide a range of individuals as the list of American taxpayers.

One of the best illustrations of the catholic nature of rose growing is seen in a typical ballot for the election of officers in the American Rose Society. Among those who ran for office one year were a surgeon, airline inspector, manufacturing process engineer, state supervisor of vocational rehabilitation, veterinarian, retired schoolteacher, retired accountant, automotive engineer, physician, dentist, retired railroad supervisor, major in the U.S. Army and a retired salesman. Roses know no boundaries. Not restricted to any social level, they are the province of everyman.

As a member of the rose fraternity you will want to share and compare your experiences with other rose growers. You will find that most rose growers feel similarly and that this common interest will open a hundred doors, a thousand doors, if you wish. The American Rose Society, the largest flower organization in existence, currently lists more than 17,500 members. Even this figure is only a visible part of the iceberg because the estimated number of rose growers in this country exceeds thirty-five million.

The hobby of rose growing can be inexpensive or expensive, depending upon your pocketbook and your enthusiasm. If you are determined to have a fair-sized rose collection but have had no experience, it would be wise to plan your plantings on paper and project them over a period of years. Start with a dozen plants and build as you learn. You may very well find yourself changing your selections as you begin to form preferences and have a chance to observe different varieties in public and private gardens.

There is a certain amount of work involved in growing roses, but you will soon find that the so-called "chores" become an excuse to be out among the roses ... that these simple acts both relax and stimulate. Every day from June till November you will find something new to marvel at. It is very difficult to remember petty vexations or the tensions of the day when you are looking at a fresh bloom with the dew still on it or at blossoms bathed in the warm light of early evening.

Part of the therapeutic value of rose growing is in the creative feeling that at times seems almost overwhelming. You may not be able to paint, draw, write or compose music but when you look at a perfect rose bloom which you grew, you know that here is something that eludes the finest artist, and *you* produced this thing of beauty. This is the mystique of the rose, something no book can explain adequately.

In her poem, *Sacred Emily*, Gertrude Stein declared, "Rose is a rose is a rose is a rose." The following chapters will explain that a rose is historic is a legend is a garden is a bouquet is a picture is forever.

I, II.   (*Opposite*) *For gardeners through the ages, a rose is a rose only when it is "American Beauty" red. Two of the best red hybrid teas available today are Bob Hope (above) and Americana (below). Bob Hope is a large-flowered vigorous plant which grows about 5 feet tall. Americana has huge blossoms at least 6 inches across, disease resistant foliage, and grows about 4 feet tall.*

III, IV, V.   *The form, color, even the perfume of the rose have been inexhaustible sources of inspiration for every kind of creative impulse. On this page are examples showing the rose on a porcelain teapot, a muffineer, and, in the form of silk blossoms, adorning a pink parasol.*

VI, VII, VIII. *Hand painting on a plate, a decorated wine cooler, and a Cabbage rose on a French tole clock honor the world's favorite flower. (Plates on both pages courtesy of McCall's Magazine.)*

IX. (Above) Canadian Centennial has been planted extensively in the rose gardens of Windsor Palace and throughout Canada in honor of its 100th anniversary in 1967.

X.   Arlene Francis is a vigorous rose, producing masses of full double flowers. When open it shows the grouping of red stamens which distinguish it from its parent Eclipse.

XI, XII. (Opposite) Moonlight Sonata—a soft apricot hybrid tea with a large flower 5½ to 6 inches, produced in profusion. Ornamental dark-green glossy foliage. Height 2½ feet. (Below) Tropicana is the only rose in history to win 14 international awards. A brilliant glowing orange-red color that holds up in the hottest days and will not fade, it is long lasting as a cut flower.

XIII. (Below) The soft shell-pink floribunda Gay Princess won the All-America Rose Selection award for 1967.

XIV. *One of two climbers developed by William Zombory of Detroit,*
Coralita is an excellent example of a fine new rose produced by an
amateur rose hybridist.

2

A ROSE IS HISTORIC

The history of the Rose
Is the history of humanity.

ANON

The rose is older than the Garden of Eden, yet today we are witnesses to the most active period in its history. On the one hand we can walk into the garden and enjoy roses that were favorites of the Caesars and on the other, marvel at the most recent introduction with the knowledge that it may be outdated within a year.

Roses were cultivated by the Chinese as early as the Shen Nung dynasty, about 2737–2697 B.C. The peak of rose culture in China is believed to have been reached between 206 B.C. and A.D. 9, during the Han dynasties.

One of the roses that exists today, as it did long before Christ, is *Rosa foetida*. We know that it was cultivated by man more than 4,000 years ago because of well-preserved wall paintings in the ruins of the Palace of Knossos on the Island of Crete. This was probably *Rosa foetida persiana*, the "Persian Yellow" rose.

Rosa damascena semperflorens, also known as the Autumn Rose and as the Rose of Four Seasons, is believed to have been grown in the Hanging Gardens of Babylon. The gardens were started during the time of Semiramis about 1200 years before the Christian Era and continued through the reign of King Nebuchadnezzar whose beautiful wife, Amytis, loved her roses above all else.

As in all eras, the rose was held in great esteem in ancient Greece. The Greek poet, Anacreon (563–478 B.C.) immortalized the rose in "The Queen of the Garden."

> If Jove would give the leafy bowers
> A Queen for all their world of flowers,
> The Rose would be the choice of Jove,
> And reign the queen of every grove.
> Sweetest child of weeping morning,
> Gem, the vest of earth adorning,

Eye of flowerets, glow of lawns,
Bud of beauty, nursed by dawns;
Soft the soul of love it breathes—
Cypria's brow with magic wreathes,
And to the zephyr's warm caresses
Diffuses all its versant tresses,
Till, glowing with the wanton's play,
It blushes a diviner ray!

Further proof of the Greeks' love for roses is to be found in the writings of Homer. He uses their colors to paint the rising of the sun in the *Iliad* and the *Odyssey*. Aurora, he said, has fingers of roses that perfume the air.

Herodotus, the Greek "Father of History," writing in the fifth century B.C., mentions fragrant roses of sixty petals that grew in Macedonia in the gardens believed to have belonged to the fabulously wealthy King Midas. Alexander the Great, King of Macedonia from 336 to 327 B.C., is credited as the first to introduce cultivated roses into Europe.

Since roses were native to contiguous countries it is difficult to accept the claim of scholars that they were not grown by the Jews and that the five references in the Bible refer to plants other than roses. King Solomon declared, "Let us crown ourselves with rose buds before they be withered." And in the Song of Solomon, "I am the Rose of Sharon and the Lily of the valleys." About 700 years later the author of the Book of Ecclesiasticus wrote: "I was exalted like a palm-tree in Engaddi, and as a rose-plant at Jericho." "Harken unto me, ye holy children, and bud forth as a rose growing by the brook of the field." Then later, "And as the flower of roses in the spring of the year."

ROSES IN EGYPT AND ROME

Though roses appear neither in the writings nor in the paintings of the ancient Egyptians, they are known to have been placed in their tombs. In a Pharaoh's tomb, excavated in 1888, was a wreath of withered roses that had been placed there 1,700 years before. A pervading rose odor may have come from long-since evaporated rose water or even from the wreath itself since the Egyptians cultivated the highly fragrant Damask Rose.

To pay the supreme compliment to Marc Antony, her Roman lover, Cleopatra spread rose petals throughout her banquet hall and covered them with a fine net so that her guest could walk on this fragrant carpet which was a cubit, or twenty inches, deep.

The Nile Valley was the source for many of the roses which the pleasure-loving Romans prized above all else. A mystery to this day is how the roses were kept fresh during the long voyage from Egypt to Rome. The trip from the mouth of the Nile to the coast of Italy took twenty days. Both the Egyptians and the Romans grew the Damask Rose, the Rose of Paestum, referred to by Virgil as *biferique rosaria Paesti*. Since it can be forced to bloom out of season the author believes that plants were grown in containers and so timed that they would burst into bloom at the end of the long journey.

Subsequently the Romans learned how to make these roses bloom in winter by growing them in hothouses in which warm water was circulated through earthenware pipes. This system became so successful that the Romans grew contemptuous of the Egyptian flowers. During the reign of Domitian the Egyptians decided to pay him the great compliment of sending rose blooms in the middle of winter. Their gesture came under the fine hone of the Roman wit, Martial. In his epigram, "To Caesar, on the Winter Roses," he mocked:

> "The ambitious inhabitants of the land watered by the Nile have sent thee, O Caesar, the roses of winter, as a present valuable for its novelty. But the boatman of Memphis will laugh at the gardens of Pharaoh as soon as he has taken one step in thy capital city—for the spring, in its charms, and the flowers in their fragrance and beauty, equal the glory of the fields of Paestum. Wherever he wanders or casts his eyes, every street is brilliant with garlands of roses. And thou, O Nile, must now yield to the fogs of Rome. Send us thy harvests, and we will send thee roses." (The Roman Chamber of Commerce must have been proud of him.)

Closely associated with Rome, the rose became a symbol of depravity so that Christians shunned it for a considerable period. Seneca derided Smyndiride, a wealthy and dissolute Sybarite, who could not sleep if a single rose petal among those with which his bed was covered, was curled. There are many accounts of prodigal Romans but the ultimate example had to be Nero. For one fete held in the Gulf of Baiae he is reported to have spent four million sesterces, about $150,000, for roses alone.

One custom, the origin of a phrase used today, was to hang a rose over a table to indicate that any conversation conducted during the meal was to be considered confidential. Hence *sub rosa*, literally "under the rose," figuratively means "in secret."

During the first century Pliny the Elder wrote his twenty-seven volume *Natural History*. In it he gave us a fascinating account of the twelve varieties of roses then known in Rome. Of their uses, he wrote:

> "The employment of the rose in chaplets (decorations), so to say, is the least use that is made of it. The flower is steeped in oil, a practice which has prevailed from the times of the Trojan war, as Homer bears witness. In addition to which it now forms an ingredient in our unguents, as mentioned on a previous occasion. It

is employed also by itself for certain medicinal purposes, and is used also to perfume the delicacies of our banquets, and is never attended with any noxious results."

EARLY SPECIES

Among the twelve varieties Pliny mentioned is the one still known as *Rosa centifolia*. "We find one variety with as many as a hundred petals and hence known as the 'centifolia.' In Italy, it is to be found in Campania, and in Greece, in the vicinity of Philippi, though this last is not the place of its natural growth."

Leaping completely over the Dark Ages to 1690 we find that the first major publication mentioning roses, *La Quintinie's Herball*, lists only 14 varieties and species of roses, but devotes space to 413 tulips. Little was published for another century until 1762, when the famous Swedish botanist, Linnaeus, still described only 14 species. In 1799, however, one botanist listed 39 species and a little later another identified 45 species. In 1825 De Candolla increased the number to 146 and in 1832 Don arrived at a total of 205 species.

As an interesting side note, considerable attention has been given recently to lavender roses, the closest approach we have made to a blue rose. The German rose, Veilchenblau, first introduced in 1909, was revived and sold a few years ago as "The Blue Rose," until the hoax was exposed. It was listed in Jackson & Perkins' catalogs fifty years ago with the notation that it was not recommended because it turned an unattractive magenta when the flowers began to die. We now have several very good lavender roses.

However, the Marquis d'Orbessan, in a paper read before the French Academy of Sciences in 1752, reported having seen blue roses growing wild near Turin. Another Frenchman, De La Neuville, stationed in Spain during the War of 1823, translated from a Spanish treatise some parts of an Arabian work indicating that the Moors, former conquerors of Spain, had cultivated blue roses which have long since disappeared. "According to Abu-el-Jair," says the translation, "there are roses of many colors—carnation white—fallow or yellow—lapis-lazuli, or sky-blue."

An Englishman is reputed to have found a blue rose in his garden, the result of a mutation. Since it was not to his liking he pulled the plant up and destroyed it. *Sic transit gloria mundi.*

2.   *(Opposite) A replica of the rose kiosk or gazebo built for the Empress Eugenie for her rose garden at Bagatelle, near Paris.*

3, 4. (Above) *The influence of the rose on pottery design is charmingly illustrated by two plates, one using the rose as a central medallion, the other as a border.*

5. (Left) *A potpourri (see Chapter 9 for recipes) could be stored in this handsome goblet. Remove the cover occasionally and enjoy the scent. Pack any surplus into small rose jars and send them as Christmas gifts.*

6. (Opposite) *The rose is the dominant theme in this collection of decorative and useful china and glassware. The small teapot at the left is Chinese and hundreds of years old; the large covered pokal, or container, to the right is primarily decorative.*

ROSE RENAISSANCE

The renaissance of the rose can be said to have begun in France when in 1804 Empress Josephine persuaded Napoleon to acquire the Chateau of Malmaison, near Paris. Here she began the first garden devoted entirely to roses. With her position and wealth she was able to gather both roses and experts. Two of the latter, the botanist, Thory, and the painter, Redouté, began work on *Les Roses,* a pictorial masterpiece devoted to the roses in Josephine's garden. She employed as chief horticulturist André Dupont, who is thought to have been the first to practice hand-pollination of roses. Despite the fact that England and France were engaged in the bitter Napoleonic Wars a British nurseryman, John Kennedy, was given a passport so he could move back and forth across the Channel to help Josephine with her rose garden, and British men-of-war were instructed to pass through their blockade any rose plants or seeds collected for Josephine. By the time of her death in 1814 she had made an interest in roses the "in" thing of her generation.

After Napoleon's exile the garden was neglected until 1910 when it was rebuilt by Jules Gravereaux, the founder of the Roseraie de l'Hay, who managed to gather 196 of the species and varieties formerly grown at Malmaison. The original collection of 250 is thought to represent all the roses then known. Among them were 167 Gallicas, 27 Centifolias, 3 Mosses, 9 Damasks, 22 Chinas, 4 Spinosissimas, 8 Albas, 3 Foetidas and 1 Musk. The species included *alpina, arvensis, banksia, carolina, cinnamonea, clinophylla, laevigata, rubrifolia, rugosa, sempervirens* and *setigera.*

Most new plants in the earlier years were those imported from foreign lands. This was true until about 1700 when a Dutch scientist discovered sex in plants, beginning the study and practice of plant breeding. Yet it was not until 1865 that the Austrian monk, Gregor Mendel, expounded his famous law of heredity. Even then it went unnoticed for several years but it is still the basis for modern genetics.

MODERN ROSES

Practically every modern rose, despite the long list of species, can trace its ancestry to four unrelated wild roses. The Cabbage or Provence rose, *R. centifolia,* imported from Asia in 1596, was crossed in 1840 with the China or Bengal rose, *R. chinensis,* that came from Central China in 1768. The result was the first hybrid perpetual. In 1867 a hybrid perpetual was crossed with the tea rose, *R. odorata,* that was brought from Southern China in 1810. One of the seedlings was *La France,* the first hybrid tea rose.

Until 1900 there were no yellow hybrid roses. Though appearing at times, yellow was an unstable element in the varieties then used in hybridization and it would always disappear under the dominant influence of the pinks. In 1900 the Frenchman, Pernet-Ducher, one of the great names in rose hybridization, crossed a red hybrid perpetual with Persian Yellow, R. *foetida persiana,* which was brought from Persia to England by Sir Henry Willcock in 1837. A milestone in rose history, his seedling was the first yellow hybrid tea, which he named Soleil d'Or. From it (in 1920) came the pure yellow Souvenir de Claudius Pernet, the first in a new strain called Pernetiana.

Three other roses that are progenitors of many of today's varieties are Mme. Caroline Testout, 1890; the still popular white hybrid perpetual, Frau Karl Druschki, 1901; and a hybrid tea that has produced a long list of seedlings and sports, Ophelia, 1913.

THE ROSE IN AMERICA

The history of the rose in America would logically begin with the forty million year old fossil found at Florissant, Colorado.

The rose played a significant part in the discovery of America. It was on October 11, 1492, that Columbus and his weary crew, while becalmed in the frightening Sargasso Sea, picked out of the water a rose branch bright with red hips. It was this that gave the seafarers the courage to continue their voyage to the New World.

The early English settlers brought with them slips of their favorite varieties but also found here many species that originated centuries before.

A century later, the American explorer, Captain John Charles Fremont, gave an almost lyrical account of roses growing in virgin prairies five hundred miles west of St. Louis. "Everywhere the Rose is met with, and reminds us of cultivated gardens and civilization. It is scattered over the prairies in small bouquets, and, when glittering in the dew and swaying in the pleasant breeze of the early morning, is the most beautiful of the prairie flowers."

Roses were loved by many of the men who forged American history. William Penn, returning from England to the colonies in 1699, was careful to include eighteen rose bushes in his luggage. George Washington planted roses at Mount Vernon and Thomas Jefferson grew them at Monticello.

ROSES IN THE WHITE HOUSE   The history of the rose in the White House began in 1800 when John Adams prudently planted a combined rose and truck garden. In 1913 Mrs. Woodrow Wilson redesigned the area outside the President's office into a formal rose garden. President Kennedy changed the garden by bringing in many other plants and even tried to change its name to the "New Flower Garden." However, tradition has prevailed and White House news dispatches usually refer to events taking place in the "Rose Garden."

In addition to the old Rose Garden which is used for receiving groups too large for indoor receptions, a new garden has been added by the East Wing which Mrs. Johnson has named the Jacqueline Kennedy Garden. It also features roses.

A prominent feature of the Rose Garden is a large magnolia tree that was planted by Andrew Jackson.

It is worth noting that roses have provided a comforting sight to our Presidents during almost two turbulent centuries and have provided an appropriate background for many historic moments.

FIRST HYBRID   The first rose to be hybridized in America was a climber that was expropriated and returned to this country under a French name. John Champneys of Charleston crossed a white musk rose with a pink Bengal. He named his seedling Champneys' Pink Cluster. However, a local florist, Philippe Noisette, sent it to his brother, Louis Noisette, of Paris. It was distributed in France in 1816 as Blush Noisette.

Another American rose that was highly regarded in Europe was the Dorothy Perkins rambler. E. Alvin Miller, the first hybridist employed by the Jackson & Perkins Company, developed this fragrant rose-pink climber that was introduced in 1901 and immediately found great favor both here and abroad. On a trip to London in 1913 the late Charles H. Perkins reported seeing "literally miles of pillars completely covered with Dorothy Perkins climbers—roses at least twenty feet high."

Where Europe was once the primary source of new roses, America has now taken the lead. Spurred by the Plant Patent Act of 1930, which provides protection for a new rose over a seventeen-year period, our hybridists began improving on perfection and have succeeded in developing a long line of superb new roses.

Four states and the District of Columbia have named the rose their official flower. Washington, D.C., settled on the American Beauty Rose, Georgia chose the white Cherokee, Iowa the wild rose, North Dakota the prairie rose and New York was content in 1958 simply to name "the rose" as its official flower. In that same year a bill was introduced in Congress by Senator Margaret Chase Smith and Representative Frances Bolton to designate the rose our national flower. The bill has been re-introduced each succeeding year and may eventually be passed.

Though roses flourish in gardens in the Southern Hemisphere, no indigenous rose has ever been found growing south of the Equator. In North America wild roses grow from Hudson Bay to the Gulf of Mexico. In 1921 the American Nature Study Society made a study of the roses native to America. Of the 200 known species (this figure varies because of disagreement among botanists) the Society found 35 that are indigenous to America.

3

A ROSE IS A LEGEND

*At the beginning of the world God created
Woman, and to please her, created the rose.*
ANON

Down through the centuries, beginning long before the written word, the rose of legend has cast its spell, influencing men and history. Because it was known to man from his very first days, the rose quite naturally became a part of ceremonial life. Its beauty and fragrance have always been a source of inspiration. No other flower has appeared more frequently in literature and few subjects have received as much attention.

Many of the rose legends sprang from attempts to explain its origin. One of the most charming of these associates the rose with creation itself. "At the beginning of the world God created Woman, and to please her, created the rose."

According to Jewish folklore the beautiful maiden, Zillah, was pursued by an obnoxious character named Hamuel. She repeatedly repelled his advances so in revenge Hamuel accused her of acts which carried the penalty of death by burning. However, when Zillah was tied to the stake the flames would not touch her but instead reached out and consumed the evil Hamuel. Then the burning brands turned into red roses and those not ignited became white roses.

A more prosaic Turkish legend tells how the first rose grew from the spot where a bead of sweat dropped from the brow of Mohammed.

One of our American legends claims that the Grant rose, with its incurving petals of blood red, sprang up at the spot where in 1836 Settler John Grant and his youthful wife and child were massacred by Seminole Indians.

A German story going back to pagan days gives the following version of the origin of the white rose. Freya, the Venus of Teutonic and northern countries, laid her veil on a red rose bush to dry. From that time on, because of her great purity, the plant produced nothing but white rose blooms.

MANY GREEK LEGENDS The Greeks were not satisfied with a single legend but

31

created many. According to one, when Aphrodite was born from sea foam a rose bush immediately appeared to perfume the air she breathed. In another legend, Apollo, while wandering through the woods, came across a nymph lying sound asleep. His kiss both awakened and terrified her. To avoid further advances she immediately turned herself into a rose. Evidently the creation of the rose was a status symbol among the early Greeks since credit was also given to other gods, including Dionysus.

INDIAN LEGENDS   From India comes the charming Hindu story of "Vishnu, Brahma and a Rose." Once upon a time Vishnu came down to earth for a visit. While he was bathing in a pool a lotus blossom opened and out stepped the god, Brahma, who proudly pointed to the lotus and claimed it to be the most beautiful flower in the world.

Vishnu agreed that it was beautiful but added, "In my paradise there is a lovelier flower, pale as the moon, with perfume so sweet that no fragrance on earth can compare with it." Unbelieving, Brahma promised that if Vishnu could prove his claim, Brahma would relinquish his position of chief god. Instantly they were transported to Vishnu's paradise where they walked through beautiful gardens to a gleaming, mother-of-pearl bower. In the center was a lone rose bush bearing a single exquisite flower. Its petals were creamy white and its fragrance was superior to anything Brahma had ever known. He bowed his head and admitted, "This is the fairest flower that grows."

ROSES AND BENEFACTION

The miracle of the rose is associated with Elizabeth, the Catholic Queen of Hungary who was canonized for her good works. It was Elizabeth's habit to give food, money and clothing to the poor but she had to do this without her husband's knowledge. On one of her errands of mercy she was suddenly met by her husband who was returning from a hunting trip. Surprised at seeing her so heavily laden he demanded to know what she was carrying. Terrified, the speechless Elizabeth clutched her cloak to conceal the gifts. But miraculously, when her husband threw it open nothing was there but red and white roses, the most beautiful he had ever seen.

In the German town of Hildesheim there grows a massive rose bush which is said to be more than eleven centuries old. It climbs up the side of a chapel originally built by Kaiser Ludwig, ruler of Germany from 814 to 840.

Above all else the Kaiser loved to hunt. One day he and his retinue came upon a magnificent white stag. The hounds broke into pursuit and because the Kaiser had the fastest horse he soon left his party far behind. The chase ended when the stag reached a stream and swam across. The Kaiser had dismounted to follow but in doing so lost his horse. When the Kaiser sounded his horn there was no answer and he finally realized he was lost.

Frightened, he took from around his neck a relic of the Holy Mother and hung it on a wild rose bush. After praying for deliverance he fell asleep. When he awoke he was amazed to find that the ground around him was covered with snow although the area beyond was green and in full blossom. The relic was frozen to the rose bush which also was in full bloom. Realizing he was witnessing a miracle, he pledged himself to erect a chapel on the spot should he be rescued. At that moment he heard hunting horns and was soon joined by his friends.

7.   *With patient and minute observations of the details of the rose, craftsmen have effectively reproduced its form in a wide variety of decorative objects.*

The Kaiser fulfilled his pledge and built the chapel beside the wild rose bush. During World War II bombing planes leveled the chapel and burned the rose bush to the ground, but it survived and today reaches thirty feet in height and covers forty feet of wall along the re-built chapel.

ROSES AND ROMANCE

A Chinese legend parallels the story of *The Emperor and His New Clothes.* As the tale goes, there was once an Emperor who had only one daughter. Her exceptional beauty attracted many suitors. To determine who would have her hand the Emperor decreed that she would be betrothed to the first man who produced a blue rose.

One suitor, a rich merchant, secretly dyed a white rose blue; another had a beautiful rose fashioned out of a blue sapphire; a third commissioned a great artist to create a blue rose of porcelain. None was found acceptable.

Then a young minstrel visited the palace and serenaded the beautiful Princess. She immediately fell in love but tearfully told him about the blue

8.   *Outstanding examples of bric-a-brac featuring the rose motif were part of the Hallmark Gallery exhibition, "The Rose." (Plates 2-8.)*

rose. The minstrel merely smiled and promised to return the next morning with a blue rose. When he appeared, the minstrel carried a white rose. The other suitors and members of the court were angry, all except the Princess. She looked at the minstrel whose eyes were filled with love and said simply, "What a beautiful blue rose."

The Emperor said, "But it is white."

She repeated, "It is a beautiful blue rose."

The Emperor not only loved his daughter but also prized her judgment more than his own. He looked at the rose and said, "If you say it is blue then it must be blue." The couple lived happily ever after.

A rose, according to an old English legend, can help a young girl find a husband. The secret is to go into the garden on midsummer's eve, pluck a rose, wrap it in clean white paper and not look at it until Christmas, when it will still be garden fresh. She is then to wear it in her bosom. The first man who plucks the rose is guaranteed to be "the future true love and husband."

Infidelity is the basis for a fable of the East that was reported by Abel Belmont in his *Dictionnaire de la Rose* (1896). While the Prophet Mohammed was waging war against the Jews his favorite wife, Aishah, took the opportunity to engage in extramarital activities with a handsome young Persian.

On his return Mohammed became suspicious and was counseled in a dream by an angel to "ask Aishah to drop an object into the pool in the center of the seraglio. If she is innocent, the object will remain unchanged; if she is guilty, it will change color." The next day Aishah was carrying a bouquet of red roses. When Mohammed asked her to dip them in the pool she was surprised but laughingly agreed. The red roses turned yellow. We are not told what color Aishah turned.

ROSES AND SEMANTICS

For those who lack eloquence the rose can be used to convey messages of love, appreciation, sympathy, congratulations and friendship, according to the Language of Flowers in which Victorians delighted.

Edmund Boyle O'Reilly put this to verse:

> The red rose whispers of passion
> The white rose breathes of love;
> Oh, the red rose is a falcon,
> And the white rose is a dove.
> I'll send you a cream-white rose bud
> With a flush in its petal tips
> For the love that is purest and sweetest
> Has the kiss of desire on its lips.

However, the code of roses seems to vary and unless both parties are tuned in on the same frequency life could become somewhat frustrating. Here is one version of the rose code.

> Red roses express love and respect
> Deep pink for gratitude and appreciation
> Light pink for admiration and sympathy
> White roses for reverence and humility
> Yellow denotes joy and gladness
> Red and yellow blends—gay and jovial
> Light blends—sociability and friendship
> Orange tones—enthusiasm and desire

In another code an entire courtship could be carried on without one spoken word. A red rose means "I love you." A white rose, "You are heavenly." If you want to say, "I'll remember you always," then send tea roses, but if you have reason to be jealous you can convey this delicately by sending an elegant yellow rose.

Again, to tell someone she is charming, graceful, pure and lovely and full of unconscious beauty, send her a floribunda cluster, a multiflora rose, a red rosebud and a burgundy rose, in exactly that order. If all fail, you had better call on Western Union.

THE INGENIOUS PHILOSOPHER   The delicacy of the rose is eloquently summed up in a story about a Persian philosopher named Zeb. It seems that Zeb was anxious to study at a Persian monastery where the members observed three rules: Think much, write a little and be as silent as possible. Zeb, hearing of a vacancy at the monastery, set out immediately to apply but arrived a day after the position had been filled by a man of wealth. The members of the monastery were mortified because Zeb, famous throughout the East, would have made a most desirable addition. The head of the monastery pondered how to convey the unpleasant news. Finally he had a cup brought and filled it with water so that one more drop would have caused it to overflow. Zeb understood the gesture and was about to retire sadly when he noticed a rose petal on the floor. He picked it up and floated it gently on top of the water so that not a drop was spilled.

This ingenious act so captivated his audience that they disobeyed the rules of the monastery and clapped their hands, whereupon the rules of admission were waived and the wise old philosopher accepted as a member.

4

A ROSE IS A GARDEN

A garden is a lovesome thing, God wot!
Rose plot,
Fringed pool,
Fern'd grot.

THOMAS EDWARD BROWN
(1830-1897)

A garden of roses is a fragrant piece of heaven. A garden without roses is a sorry thing.

While some would consider these statements prejudiced a vast number of people would not. It is small wonder that more than thirty-five million American homeowners grow roses. What other plant has the versatility of the rose with its varying colors, fragrance and abundance of perfect flowers all season long? It can be used alone as a specimen plant, in groups, in combination with other plants, in foundation plantings or in the over-all home landscaping.

How could anyone provide a more friendly and inviting approach to a home than a low picket fence ablaze with climbing roses and at the end of the path a doorway framed by hybrid tea and floribunda roses? Even an anonymous rented house or an occasionally used vacation cabin can acquire personality when given such a treatment.

The ways to use roses are legion. Some ideas are illustrated in the drawings and pictures accompanying this chapter.

On the assumption that you have never grown roses—here are some of the fundamentals that will help guide you along the road to a truly wonderful adventure.

HOW TO BUY A ROSE

First, the plant. No doubt you will hear stories about people who bought bargain roses and had wonderful results. You will never hear from those who bought bargain roses and were disappointed. Frequently, bargain roses are plants that have been discarded by greenhouse growers. These plants have an understock that is suitable for greenhouse growing but unsatisfactory for garden use. The wisest move is to give yourself an even break and start with good plants.

When you examine the catalogs of reputable nurseries you will find that they offer only #1 grade, two-year-old, field-grown roses. The three grades in roses, #1, #1½ and #2, are based on the number of stems and their length. A #1, which is the only type of plant you should consider, is as follows:

Hybrid tea, three or more stems 18 inches or longer, branching no more than 3 inches from the bud union (the knob at ground level).

Floribunda, three or more 15-inch stems; *climbers,* the same as floribundas except that the stems should be at least 24 inches long.

Prices range from $1.50 for non-patented roses to $4.00 for the latest introductions which, because they are new, may be in short supply.

LEARN TYPES OF ROSES

The extent to which you will have to study fundamentals will depend upon the direction your hobby will ultimately take. But even if you intend to plant and enjoy only a few rose bushes, it still is important to know the types of plants that can be used before deciding upon specific varieties. And before selecting varieties you would be wise to learn the characteristics and qualities of roses so that you can exercise some judgment in your purchases. Should you decide later to try your hand at hybridizing then you must know not only how to judge a plant but also how to describe it to the satisfaction of the patent office. (See Chapter 7.)

The first step is to decide the type of rose or roses you need. Types are determined by growth habits. Under any one type you will have a choice of a vast number of named varieties. The qualities to be judged in choosing varieties will be discussed later.

The basic types of roses you need be concerned with are Hybrid Teas, Floribundas, Climbers, Species and Old-Fashioned roses (as differentiated from modern). You may read or hear about Hybrid Perpetuals, Tea, Polyantha and

9. (*Opposite, above*) *The hybrid tea occasionally produces several buds on one stem, but the classic form is a large single flower at the end of a long stem. After this flower is spent, the next one will grow from the first five-leaflet leaf below it. The beginning of new flowers can be seen at the axil of the leaves on the right side of the stem in the middle and at the bottom of the picture.*

10. (*Opposite, below*) *The floribunda typically produces a large candelabra cluster of flowers that begins with a single terminal bud and then rapidly spreads out to the laterals.*

Grandiflora roses. Grandiflora is a term describing a tall-growing Floribunda. The British refuse to accept the term. They feel there is no need for it. There also are specialized types such as Miniatures and Tree or Standard roses.

HYBRID TEA   Hybrid tea roses resulted from breeding hybrid perpetuals with tea roses. They bloom from June to November and produce large flowers on single stems. Plants average from 3 to 6 feet depending upon the climate. They can be used in a foundation planting and are most effective when combined with the more heavily flowered floribunda. More frequently they are used in rose beds and flower gardens. When required for use indoors they are generally planted in a cutting garden where constant color is not a factor. The flowers are long stemmed and are ideal for flower arrangements.

FLORIBUNDA   Formerly known as large-flowered hybrid polyanthas, floribundas are lower growing than hybrid teas but more disease-resistant and hardier. They are free-flowering and can be counted on as a constant source of color which makes them effective where mass color is required, as in a low hedge. Though their flowers are smaller than the hybrid teas new varieties of floribundas are being bred that produce ever larger blooms. Flowers appear both on single stems and on large candelabra-like clusters that bloom principally in June. Even if blossoms are cut for the house color will be left in the garden. The height of the floribunda is usually from 2 to 3 feet but it is considerably higher in warm and sub-tropical areas.

CLIMBERS   Climbers vary from those that trail over the ground, to make flowering ground covers, to the pillar type whose strong canes grow straight up from 6 to 8 feet and can be used to hide an ugly post, to the more usual type that cover trellises, fences and doorways, and provide a brilliant splash of color.

Some of the older climbers bloom only in June but the modern varieties are repeat bloomers and can be counted on for colorful blossoms during the entire season. The biggest show is in June with autumn a close second and recurring flowers during the intervening months. Again, geographical location will affect their height which can range from 6 to 25 feet.

11.   (*Opposite, above*) *Climbers can be pruned to keep them at the required height, but consider their growth habit when you buy. Varieties such as Royal Gold would be fine for a low fence such as this.*

12.   (*Opposite, below*) *A vertical garden. Two vigorous plants produced this abundance of bloom!*

TRAINING CLIMBERS

If the walls of the house are wood it is a simple matter to screw in some eye hooks through which plastic clothesline can be threaded to provide an inconspicuous framework on which canes of the climbers can be trained. For brick, stone, or stucco houses where it is impossible to insert eye hooks, a series of wooden trellises set in the ground will provide the same results.

Train center canes to form a graceful vertical curve, bend the outer canes into a more or less horizontal position and then fill in the area between with the remaining canes. Be sure to leave room for the shoots that the horizontal canes will send straight up. The total effect will be most pleasing and will give all the buds an opportunity to develop into full flowers. Use string when tieing the canes to the framework. Avoid wire since canes move about in the wind and wire, even the flower arrangers' twistems, will either cut the cane in two or cause bruises that encourage disease.

13.   *A modern version of* treillage *(back in high style again) is made from branches of bamboo to which climbing roses are tied with green string.*

14. *An arbor covered with fragrant climbing roses makes an ideal spot for a garden bench.*

15. *(Above) An upright post in this split-rail fence is completely hidden by a single plant of the climber Aloha. This variety is never leggy but is covered with blossoms from top to bottom.*

16. *(Opposite) Although the ornate archways are extremely high, climbing roses have no difficulty reaching the top.*

CLIMBERS FOR ARCHES, WALLS AND TRELLISES

17.   (*Opposite, above*) *Four vigorous climbers provide a lot of blossoms!*

18.   (*Opposite, below*) *The bright red of the climber Blaze and the white of floribunda Summer Snow make this truly a picture window.*

19.   (*Above*) *A wagon wheel provides an unusual trellis for this climbing rose.*

20. *Old-fashioned hybrid rugosa Max Graf, hardy and vigorous, is excellent in rock gardens, for covering a bank, or along steps. The flowers, bright pink with golden centers, come in June and do not repeat. Rugosas are shrub roses with rugose or deeply wrinkled leaves. If you are tired of the ubiquitous weigela or spirea hedges, try the rugosas (far more practical than the highly advertised Rosa multiflora), or use them as a background planting for the smaller roses.*

SPECIES ROSES   Species roses are the native or wild roses from which all hybrids originated. Most species bloom only in June and generally have small, five-petaled flowers. Many are hardier than the hybrids and are less susceptible to insects and diseases. They have a definite charm and sometimes can be used effectively in landscape planning because of their foliage, fruits and autumn color.

In this country perhaps 50 of the 200 or so that exist can be obtained from nurserymen. A recommended selection, though not necessarily inclusive, follows in Chapter 5 with the lowest zone (see Plant Zone Hardiness Map, also in Chapter 5) in which they will grow.

OLD-FASHIONED ROSES   These varieties include hybrid perpetuals and tea roses developed during the last century. They are valued mostly for their quaintness or as collectors' items.

TREE ROSES   Also known as standards, they are named varieties of floribundas or hybrid tea roses budded at the top of straight, heavy canes. They are usually 3 to 4 feet high and add height to rose beds, provide color accents in the garden and are frequently used in formal plantings. Tree roses are highly vulnerable to freezing temperatures and require special protection during cold winters.

The striking appearance of tree roses makes them the center of interest in any garden. Producing perfect flowers at eye level, they can be used to add height to a rose bed, or a single bush can be used as an accent plant. They are most striking when used in columns beside a pathway.

21.   *Tree roses or standards may be budded with hybrid teas, floribundas, grandifloras, climbers, etc. and the bloom is determined by the variety selected. Although they require special care in cold areas (see page 85), they make handsome accent plants. Here they add height to a bed of hybrid teas.*

22. *Low-growing floribundas edge beds of hybrid teas in a formal rectangular garden. A tree rose focuses attention on the pool.*

MINIATURES Miniature roses average 12 inches in height and have perfectly shaped blooms that are often scarcely bigger than a pencil eraser. The bushy plants produce flowers profusely. Winter hardy, they are effective in rock gardens, window boxes and as edgings for floribunda beds. Only a few colors are now available but these are being extended with new introductions each year.

ROSES INDOORS

Unless you own a greenhouse it is hopeless to try to grow garden roses indoors. It just won't work.

Some people are successful in growing miniatures indoors but they are not for the neophyte or for the person who wants flowers and greenery without too much effort.

The requirements: First, the plant must be placed near a window with southern exposure since miniatures need all the sun they can get. The foliage requires a humid atmosphere which can be supplied by placing the pot in the middle of a pie pan or shallow dish filled with small stones. Keep this filled with water that can evaporate and provide the necessary humidity. Whenever the soil becomes dry, water the plants at the top of the pot. In addition, they need liquid feeding, a regular spraying program to prevent disease, and occasional syringing of foliage. Some would consider the problem a challenge but most would agree that indoor miniatures require just too much effort.

It is generally recommended that those who buy miniature roses at the March flower shows enjoy the first blooms indoors, but then by late March plant the roses in the garden (tap them out of the pot first) and leave them there. Since they are completely winter-hardy they will continue to produce well in the garden for many years.

23, 24.   *Blossoms from miniature roses, though perfectly formed, are seldom larger than a thimble. The plants are winter hardy and are excellent for rock gardens or window boxes. Baby Betsy McCall and Ruby Jewel are shown.*

ROSE GARDENS IN PLANTERS

25, 26, 27, 28. *City dwellers with limited space find container gardens highly practical because they use minimum soil, provide a clean and compact appearance, and are easy to water, feed, weed and prepare for winter. Further, when rose plants are in-between blooming, they may be replaced by others in full bloom.*

When the Museum of Modern Art in New York City first opened its sculpture garden, the only source of color in the entire area were the floribundas Fashion, shown here in simple but attractive stone flower pots.

PLANNING A HYBRID TEA GARDEN

Hybrid tea roses are best used in a bed located where it can be seen from the house or terrace so you can enjoy their color and fragrance whether indoors or out.

If you prefer a semi-formal or formal garden draw up a plan and build it by adding a few plants each year. Within a season or two your garden will begin to take form and will eventually give you the effect you want. In a cutting garden (used to provide flowers for inside the home) you may prefer to have one each of many varieties. But in a display garden it is more effective to use several plants of one variety, grouping them among other roses with harmonizing colors.

A rectangular formal garden can be made with four "L"-shaped beds that enclose a central circular planting. This can be achieved by planting one bed at a time over five years, placing minimum strain on the back and pocketbook.

Drawing 1.   *Plant your roses where they can be enjoyed most. This bed of hybrid teas and floribundas is notched right into the edge of the paving.*

29. *This formal rose garden was planned before it was planted and grew with the years.*

For ease of maintenance, make the "L"-shaped beds no more than 3 feet wide. This will allow a double row of bushes which should be staggered to get the maximum use of space. Again, by quartering the circular bed with paths, you can get in close enough to enjoy individual flowers and handle the watering, spraying and other chores without difficulty.

Drawing 2.   *(Opposite, left) A split-level house features a climber on the garage door and roses along the driveway.*

Drawing 3.   *(Opposite, right) Plant roses in beds and borders on the terrace and in the garden, alone and combined with other flowers.*

30.   *Climbing roses and floribundas bring color, fragrance and privacy to a terrace.*

31.   *(Opposite) Slow-growing, small-leaved boxwood can be trimmed to form a dense low hedge, an ideal border for roses.*

32. *In the New Jersey garden of Mrs. Lewis M. Hull, a sundial is framed by the hybrid tea rose Peace, probably the most popular of all roses. The hedge is boxwood.*

33. *(Opposite) Two tree roses frame a rear entrance. Because of the camera angle, they appear higher than they are. The height of tree roses is determined at the time they are bedded and never varies. Usually they are standardized at 3 to 4 feet. They are sometimes grown lower but never higher.*

CASUAL ROSE GARDENS

However, a formal garden that requires a fair-sized piece of property is not essential. A small curving bed or semi-circular planting can be placed at the corner of the house combining hybrid teas or floribundas with plants that will provide color and form during the months when roses are not in bloom. For instance, plant evergreens for winter and flowering shrubs, with tulips and daffodils, for springtime color. If you want to edge off the planting try boxwood (trimmed low), to hide the base of the rose plants while they are not in flower: Dusty Miller will give a neat effect and sweet alyssum will provide both color and fragrance.

Perhaps the most useful type of rose is the floribunda. It has a wide range of color, size, fragrance and type of foliage. For any problem spot there is almost certainly a floribunda to fill it. Its habit of growth and mass color make

34. *Shrub roses and some hardy varieties that thrive with minimum care can be interspersed among annuals and perennials in a flower border. Spikes of delphiniums contrast in color and form.*

35. *Belgian blocks provide an effective border and gravel chips pre-*
vent the growth of weeds in the path.

the floribunda ideal for foundation plantings, living hedges, border plantings, or as a colorful accessory of plantings for such garden structures as flagpoles, bird-houses, mailboxes and birdbaths. It is best to group three or more bushes of the same variety. The total effect is far superior to a mixture of colors.

Floribundas and miniatures are used for borders and may also be combined to good effect in planters such as redwood boxes, cement urns and modern ceramic and plastic pots.

A trellis, fence or stone wall will be infinitely more attractive if a few climbers are trained on it. The flowers and foliage, which soften the bare effect, will give your property new interest and beauty. Pillar-type climbers will shoot up sturdy stems and abundant foliage to clothe a washing-line pole and at the same time provide large hybrid tea-shaped flowers for cutting purposes. Taller climbers can be used to frame a door, grace a garage wall or even to climb three stories high to provide a curtain of foliage and flowers and cut the glare from a bare white wall.

36. Poised against a broad enclosing wall, roses fill a gap and bring grace and charm to a small space.

37. (Opposite, above) The floribunda Golden Garnette stays uniformly low so that it may be used as a colorful edging for a terrace or porch.

38. (Opposite, below) A serpentine masonry wall is softened effectively with an edging of All-America floribunda Vogue, a good choice where a rose with a neat, restrained habit is required.

39, 40. *(Opposite, above) A wooden fence is a marvelous foil for roses. All-America floribunda Ivory Fashion, left; white hybrid tea John F. Kennedy, right.*

41. *(Opposite, below) A curved border of roses dramatizes the lawn, softens the foundations of the house and unifies foreground and background areas.*

42. *A large placid lake and a planting of the heavily-flowered floribunda rose Fashion—with its coral-pink, long-lasting blossoms against the gray rock—make an unforgettable picture.*

COLOR HARMONY

Color harmony and contrast should be considered when selecting varieties for foundation plantings or garden combinations. The range of colors available among roses is probably wider than that of any other plant. Besides the basic reds, yellows, pinks and whites there are many other colors such as coral, bi-colors and even lavender, brown and green, though few are likely to choose the green rose, *Rosa chinensis viridiflora*, except as an oddity.

Color harmony is easier on the eyes, generally, but a sharp color contrast can also be effective. In rose gardens where there is plenty of room for beds the best and safest method is to use only one variety in each bed, or to group like colors together. When a tree rose is used in a bed for height it is often better to choose a color that contrasts with the flowers in the bed.

Deep reds should be kept separate from dark backgrounds where they tend to become lost. Use them against white, yellow or light pink varieties.

The scarlet or flame colors can be used safely with warm pinks and also combine well with yellows and oranges.

Drawing 4.   *Use hybrid teas in island plantings on a large paved terrace. Their fragrance and color will be appreciated there.*

Pale yellow, white and cream tones harmonize with almost any other color and are therefore completely safe with the most vivid carmine pinks, terra cotta and orange roses.

Rather than planting salmon pinks with light pinks, whites or yellows, try using them with shades of rich orange, cerise or flame. Pale pinks give a pleasing effect when combined with dark red or crimson roses. Usually it is preferable to blend the soft pinks with brighter colors to provide contrast.

A restful effect can be achieved by grouping the softer or paler shades but where an accent or focal point is required, mass the brighter colored varieties.

The idea that roses should be set apart from other flowers has long since been disproved. They can and should be used in the general landscaping and in foundation plantings.

The most important factor in planning home landscaping is to settle first on your objectives. Then it is a simple matter to decide whether to use hybrid tea, floribunda, climber or tree roses and to decide on a color scheme. In this way your roses will become an integral part of the over-all design.

The drawings illustrate varied garden designs featuring roses.

Drawing 5.   *Assure privacy for the outdoor lounge with climbing roses trained on a screen trellis. Floribunda roses are a natural choice to plant between the terrace and the house wall.*

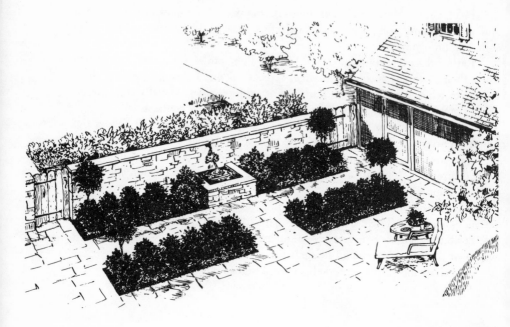

Drawing 6. *Hybrid tea, floribunda and grandiflora roses are combined in the beds and borders of a terrace rose garden, with tree roses as accents.*

Drawing 7. *You cannot beat a climber for covering an arbor or pergola.*

70

5

GROWING ROSES
SUCCESSFULLY

Dig a trench a foot deep...the ground is dug deeper for roses than for crops.

PLINY, THE ELDER
23-79 A.D.

E ven the average homeowner who has little or no knowledge of gardening can grow magnificent roses. Time and effort are involved, though neither need be excessive. As in anything else, extra care and diligence have their rewards and the end result is one of matchless beauty.

The quality of rose blooms varies according to seasons, parts of a season, or between one climatic area and another. Perhaps the best guide to successful rose growing is to understand the qualities of the ideal rose climate. It is virtually unattainable, but if even one step can be taken to bring growing conditions closer to the ideal, better roses will result. Don't worry about compromises because even if you miss the mark by 50 percent you will still be happy with the roses you grow.

SELECT SITE TO MEET PLANT NEEDS

SUN   Roses need at least six hours of sun each day. Morning sun is particularly valuable because it dries off foliage and helps prevent mildew. While sunlight should be of moderate intensity, there is no possibility of too much sunlight if temperatures are moderate. In fact, the more sunlight the better the plants will grow. However, flowers open and fade more rapidly and colors tend to bleach under intense sunlight. So filtered sunlight during the hottest part of the day will prolong the life of blooms and delay fading.

TEMPERATURE   The ideal temperature range is 65 to 70 degrees F. during the day and 50 to 60 degrees at night. Evaporation and transpiration of water from plant tissues increases as the temperature of the soil rises to about 70 degrees. Here again, filtered shade, from trees or structures during the hottest part of the day, will alleviate excessive heat.

73

However, wide variations between night and day temperatures pose another problem. If nights are cold and days hot, the root intake of water will not balance moisture loss because the soil warms much more slowly than the air. A mulch provides an easy solution because it keeps the soil warmer at night and cooler during the day.

Plentiful snow in the winter is a great boon. Often referred to by farmers as "the poor man's mulch," snow provides excellent insulation against cold and prevents the "heaving" or moving of soil during freeze-and-thaw periods. The insulating qualities of snow are best illustrated by the Eskimo igloo in which a candle or two can provide all the heat necessary for human life.

HUMIDITY   Low humidity and wind are probably most critical because the combination is the worst culprit for causing plant tissues to dry out. Plants exposed to high humidity but sheltered from the wind are able to flourish in temperatures above 100 degrees. However, humidity close to the saturation point combined with temperatures near 70 degrees tend to produce conditions favorable to mildew. The ideal humidity level should not rise above 75 to 80 percent. Air circulation is the best control for high humidity and protection from strong winds is the remedy for low humidity.

AIR   A windbreak between the roses and the prevailing winds will reduce this hazard but there should be a "gate" of some kind to allow enough wind to come into the garden and provide the necessary air circulation. The ideal area would have no strong winds, only gentle breezes moving freely among the rose plants. Plant roses away from large trees or shrubs that would deprive them of the air, sun and food they need.

WATER   Plenty of water is essential for healthy plants and large luscious blooms. The ideal climate would provide about 2 inches of rain weekly. It should be gentle to minimize danger to blooms and to ensure that all the rain is absorbed by the soil gradually. Whenever the weekly rainfall falls short of the minimum 2 inches, it should be supplemented. Try to water while there is still plenty of sunshine to dry off the leaves. Or, better still, use a water wand or a canvas soaker to avoid wetting the foliage.

Though roses require lots of moisture, their roots will not tolerate standing in stagnant water. If drainage is poor it should be rectified when the rose bed is prepared. The need for drainage can be determined easily when the hole is dug. Pour some water in and if it does not drain off readily line the bottom of the bed with a generous layer of coarse stone or shards from broken flower pots.

Do not plant under eaves. Ice and water could damage the plant.

SOIL   The best soil for roses is loose, well aerated and fertile. For every two shovelfuls of soil mix in thoroughly a shovelful of peat moss. This will take care of the aeration. Well-rotted manure, if available, or compost will do wonders for poor soil. Where the soil is predominantly sand, mix in one-third loam and compost. If it is mainly clay, add sand until the soil becomes friable, or workable. Rose beds should be dug a minimum of 18 inches and preferably 24 inches deep.

PLANTING TIME

For the best time to plant bare-root or potted rose plants consult the area planting guide in Chapter 14.

Some gardeners prefer potted rose plants because they may be planted later in the season. Also the buyer can see the type of plant and know that it is alive. However, bare-root plants are preferable since there is no container to restrict the root system which should be free to spread out and reach all available moisture and food.

WHEN THE ROSES COME   Remove roses from package and place roots in a pail of water until you can plant—up to 1 week if necessary. Keep pail out of sunlight.

If it is not convenient to soak the roses as soon as the mailman brings them, open the carton and inspect the polyethylene bag. If it has not been punctured, there is no urgency about soaking the roses. If the bag has any holes in it, get the roots into a pail of water immediately. The worst thing that can happen— usually fatal—is to allow the plant to dry out.

One way or another, however, be sure the roots get a thorough soaking before you plant.

HOW TO PLANT BARE-ROOT ROSES

Be sure the hole is wide enough to allow the roots to spread out naturally in all directions. Prune any broken roots just above the damaged area. Also cut off the tip end of all roots to force new growth of feeder roots. Using the prepared soil mixture, build a cone in the center of the hole. When the plant is seated on top of the cone the knob just above the roots, known as the "bud union," should be at ground level in temperate areas, 2 inches above ground in warm climates and 2 inches below ground in cold regions. The level can easily be determined by resting the shovel handle across the top of the hole.

Add more soil until the hole is three-quarters full, packing it closely around the roots to eliminate air pockets. Step into the hole and stamp the soil down firmly as added insurance. Now fill the hole with water. After this has drained, fill the rest of the hole with soil and use the balance to build a 6- to 8-inch mound around the base of the plant. Finally, prune off all canes about an inch above the mound.

43, 44. (*Opposite, above*) The knob or graft union (*top of white root*) should be at ground level in temperate areas, two inches above ground in warm climates and two inches below ground in cold regions. After soil has been firmly packed around the roots, a bucket of water will not only give the plant a good start but will also help to eliminate any possible air pockets among the roots.

45, 46. (*Opposite, below*) Pack the soil firmly around the root system. Hill up the soil and mulch around the base of the plant to prevent the plant from drying out before new growth begins.

47, 48. (*Right*) After new growth is approximately two inches long, spread fertilizer in a circle around plant, being careful not to have any touch the canes. Scratch it lightly into the soil and then water well. A water wand prevents hose pressure from displacing soil and also prevents water from splashing onto the foliage, where it can cause mildew.

49. (Left) When dusting plants it is wise also to dust the soil around the plant as well as underneath the leaves.

50. (Below) A generous layer of mulch will keep the soil cool during the day and warm at night, and also conserve moisture.

51. (Opposite) After the first frosts of fall, hill up the soil 6 to 8 inches around the base of the plant.

LATE PLANTING Should you be forced to plant bare-root roses late in the season, say during May in New York State, the danger of stems drying out is more critical. This can be avoided very simply. Instead of hilling up soil, cover the plants loosely with wet burlap and keep it constantly moist until new growth appears. Then remove the burlap in the late afternoon and replace it only to protect the new growth from very hot sun.

Keep in mind that dry air is a plant's worst enemy. Protect the plants from wind and sun while planting. Be sure there are no air pockets around the roots. These will prevent the intake of water necessary for growth of new feeder roots, retarding the growth of your rose bush. The soil mound at the base of the plant will prevent the canes from drying out before the plant begins active growth.

PLANTING POTTED ROSES

If the plant is in a can, ask your nurseryman to slit the sides. Tar-paper pots will tear off easily. Dig the hole twice the depth of the pot so that the bottom soil is well loosened. Carefully remove the plant from the pot, taking care not to jar the root system. Replace enough soil so that the graft union is at ground level and pack the remaining soil around the root ball leaving a 4-inch saucer. Again, be sure to avoid air pockets. Fill the saucer with water and after it has drained off, fill the balance of the hole with soil and apply a mulch.

SPACING

Plant hybrid tea roses 24 inches apart and floribundas 18 inches apart. This allows plants to branch out properly and have sufficient room for air circulation.

LABELING

All plants arrive with a metal name plate that is attached to the bush with thin wire. These should be removed for two reasons. The wire will rust and the label will fall off, or it may be on a stem that is cut off. The most important reason is that as the stems grow larger the wire may very easily girdle the cane and kill it.

Since the metal plates have a small hole through which the wire is threaded, it is a simple matter to thumbtack the plate to a small wooden stake. The stake should be placed near the bush when it is planted since it is easy to misplace the marker and forget the name of the variety. Knowing the names of your roses adds to the enjoyment of growing them and helps you to determine which varieties grow best in your garden.

AFTER-CARE

When new growth appears on the canes above the soil mound and is about a quarter-inch long, remove a quarter of the mound soil. When it is a half-inch long, reduce the mound by half and when the growth is a full inch, carefully take away the balance of the soil. In this way the canes are protected against drying out and from injury due to late freezes.

FEEDING

Note that nothing has been said about fertilizer. More roses are damaged by over-feeding than under-feeding. Allow freshly planted bare-root roses to establish their root systems at their own rate. Do not use plant food until the plants are fully covered with foliage. Then use an all-purpose rose food following carefully the directions on the package. Spread the food in a circle about 6 inches from the stem and scratch it into the soil. Then water well so that the food will get down to the roots.

XV, XVI. (*Top, left*) *Royal Gold, a vigorous climber and* (*right*) *Don Juan, excellent on a pillar.*

XVII. (*Left*) *A showy climber, Dr. J. H. Nicolas has upright canes which grow close to pillars and posts.*

XVIII. (*Right*) *The floribunda Betty Prior can be pruned medium low as a hedge plant or can be allowed to grow tall as a shrub. Very hardy, it requires minimum care.*

XIX. *In the Massachusetts garden of Frederick Beinecke, Canterbury bells in tones of blue, lavender and purple are a contrast to brilliant red climbing roses.*

XX. *(Opposite) Orchid Masterpiece is popular in the gardens of flower arrangers.*

XXI.   *Brilliant red roses are always favored by gardeners. World's Fair Salute was chosen as the 1964 Rose of the Year.*

XXII, XXIII.   *(Opposite) And of all the red climbers, Blaze is by far the most popular. One sees it blooming all over America.*

XXIV. *Hawaii has orange-coral blooms about 6 inches across with a definite raspberry scent. Its glossy leaves show a tint of red in the fall. Very prolific, and popular with flower arrangers.*

XV.   *Polynesian Sunset is deep coral with huge 6½-inch double flowers*
* long stems, making them ideal for cutting. The Jackson & Perkins test*
* nel of home gardeners named it Rose of the Year for 1965.*

XXVI. (Above) A consistent high scorer in the American Rose Society's annual trials is the floribunda Fashion which provides a solid bed of color on both sides of the path. In the foreground is the hybrid tea New Yorker.

XXVII. (Below) A delightful corner garden featuring the All-America hybrid tea King's Ransom in the foreground, and Pigmy Red as an edging plant for the pool.

Only two more feedings will be needed during the season. Apply the second when the first blooms have reached their peak and the third feeding in early August. There should be no plant food remaining to force continued active growth when the first frosts arrive and the plant is ready to enter its winter period of dormancy.

Vary this feeding schedule for established plants. They should receive the first feeding in early spring when new growth is about an inch long. The second and third feedings are given at the same time as above.

Another method of feeding that is finding wide acceptance because of its ease of operation is foliar feeding. After the initial ground feeding in early spring the entire feeding schedule can be handled while spraying for pests and diseases. Every other week add 2 teaspoonfuls of Rapidgro per gallon of all-purpose spray and continue until early August.

PRUNING

Cutting flowers for indoor use is a form of pruning; it induces more stem growth and increases flower production. However, do not cut so severely that by removing too much of its foliage you put a strain on the plant. When you cut a flower be sure that at least two sets of five-leaflet leaves remain. Cut off just above the upper five-leaflet leaf. A new stem will grow out of the axil of the top leaf. To keep the bush properly shaped and avoid criss-crossing stems in the center of the plant, select leaflets that face out.

In the spring, before new growth has begun, cut off any wood that shows signs of winterkill (blackened canes) or that appears to be diseased. If you desire early flowers, leave all the green wood you can find. But if you are willing to wait a little longer in return for a bushier plant, prune hybrid tea canes to within 6 to 8 inches of ground level and cut floribundas to 12 to 15 inches.

Drawing 8.

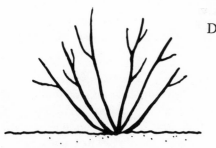

Hybrid tea unpruned.   *Hybrid tea properly pruned.*

Drawing 9.

Florbunda unpruned.

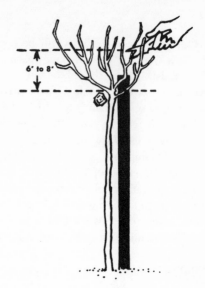

6' to 8'

12"- 15"

Floribunda properly pruned.

Drawing 10. *Prune tree roses as you do hybrid teas, cutting the branches to within six to eight inches of the crown (top of trunk) to encourage a compact, vigorous new growth. Tree roses should be pruned immediately after they are set upright in the spring.*

PRUNING CLIMBERS Prune everblooming climbers in the fall. Remove at the base the canes that bore flowers during the summer but carefully preserve the new shoots because these will be the source of flowers the following season. After flowers are spent, cut them off so they won't go to seed but be careful not to remove foliage as new flowers will come from the top set of leaves. If you cut flowers for the house leave at least two sets of five-leaflet leaves on the stem.

With single-flowering climbers remove the old wood at the base as soon as the blooming period ends, again preserving the new wood that will produce flowers the following year.

SUCKERS Barring species roses and miniatures, all garden roses are the amalgamation of two types of roses, a wild plant that supplies the root system and the named variety that has been grafted onto the wild plant. The point of demarcation is the knob known as the graft union. Sometimes new growth comes up from the wild plant below the graft union. Unless it is immediately controlled it will take over and replace the hybrid. Control is very simple. Any time a new shoot clearly stems from below the graft union either scrape it off with a trowel or merely get a good hold and yank it off. If caught early these shoots tear away easily and cause no damage. To prune them above ground is only to invite the production of more shoots.

CULTIVATION

If no mulch is used (see below) it will be necessary to cultivate the soil around the plants. This simply means scratching the surface soil occasionally so that it never bakes into a hard crust. Do not cultivate deeply or you may injure roots near the surface.

MULCHES

A 2- to 3-inch layer of mulch will help reduce weeds, preserve moisture, prevent splashing of fungus-infected soil onto plant leaves and serve as climate control by keeping the soil cool in summer and warm in winter.

Do not use grass cuttings because they tend to produce fungus diseases. Salt hay, corn cobs, peat moss or buckwheat hulls may be used. The last makes for a tidier bed. If peat moss is used do not allow it to cake on the surface or it will prevent rain and water from soaking through.

PESTS AND DISEASES

Since it is far easier to prevent diseases than to cure them, it is wise to spray or dust plants from early spring till fall with an all-purpose formulation. Begin as soon as foliage is fully out and continue once a week, or as soon as possible after a rainfall. If this schedule is followed faithfully you can forget about all diseases and pests except possibly the Japanese beetle. If your all-purpose spray or dust is not effective against Japanese beetles us a DDT spray. The most direct method is simply to pick the beetles off the flowers and drop them into a can of kerosene. (One youngster working at the rate of ten beetles a cent can keep everybody happy.)

Some specific diseases and pests together with recommended control measures are as follows:

Blackspot This is a fungus disease that affects leaves. It begins on older leaves as small fuzzy black spots which quickly expand, causing the leaves to turn yellow and die. The loss of foliage can seriously weaken or kill a plant. Control: In addition to spraying or dusting the plants on a regular schedule, the infected leaves should be cleaned up and burned.

Powdery Mildew Also a fungus disease, mildew is spread by the wind; it thrives best under still, humid conditions and cool nights. Leaves become wrinkled and show blisters covered with white powder. At times, buds, flowers and stems are also affected.
Control: Use an all-purpose dust or spray weekly.

Cankers   Spreading spots of red, tan, white, purple or brown form on the canes and cause dieback when they completely girdle the stem.
Control: Use an all-purpose dust or spray; prune back to clean wood in spring.

Crown Gall   Caused by bacteria, this is a swelling tumor that forms near the graft union. There is no definite cure. Remove infected plants and burn them, replace the soil with uninfected soil and sterilize contaminated tools.

Aphids   Tiny lice that swarm over buds and tender new growth. They feed by sucking, causing distorted petals and flowers.
Control: An all-purpose spray or dust controls them easily.

Thrips   Very tiny, these insects appear as yellow specks on rosebuds which become deformed, or fail to open.
Control: Easily prevented by weekly spraying or dusting.

Borers   These are the maggots or grubs of adult insects such as bees, beetles and wasps. The larvae are laid inside cut stems. When they bore into the cane they cause dieback.
Control: Sealing off the end of the stems with tree wound paint, especially from midsummer on, is the best preventive but spraying and dusting also help.

Japanese Beetles   The larvae of this well-known pest develop under grass sod. Easily identified, the mature beetles are a quarter-inch long and have a metallic green color. They devour both leaves and flowers but especially the latter.
Control: A lawn application of chlordane will control the population in the immediate area. For those that fly in, frequent spraying with DDT will help. Otherwise the best cure is to pick the beetles off the plants and drop them into a can of kerosene.

ORGANIC GARDENING

Since the publication of Rachel Carson's book, *Silent Spring,* a great many gardeners have turned away from all chemicals and practice organic gardening. The theory, basically sound, is that a healthy plant is the best defense against insects and diseases. I feel that organic gardening can be carried to extremes, causing unnecessary work by denying the use of beneficial and safe chemicals. It would be comparable in medicine to the refusal to use antibiotics, vaccines or any of the benefits of medical research that have done so much to improve health and lengthen life.

However, there are many ways in which organic gardening makes good sense. In preparing the rose bed the organic gardener will dig down 30 inches and add rich loamy soil plus compost, rotted manure and rock phosphate. Each spring more rotted manure is added to the top layer of soil. Mulches play an important part in organic gardening. They are used to retain moisture, to reduce weeds and for temperature control in the soil.

In lieu of chemicals the organic gardener trusts to the strength of the plant and to natural enemies to control insect infestation. One method used to control aphids is to buy ladybirds (relatively inexpensive) and set them free among the roses. Not all are released simultaneously since once the supply of insects has been devoured, the ladybirds move on to greener pastures. The praying mantis is a natural enemy of Japanese beetles.

To those organic gardeners who are not familiar with purple martins, a single bird is said to consume 2,000 insects a day and their habit is to live in colonies. J. L. Wade of Griggsville, Illinois has taken on the purple martins as a personal crusade and has devised a birdhouse that the finicky martins approve of. It can be raised and lowered for cleaning since martins will not abide a dirty house. One version will handle 12 families and another 36 families. Once the martins have adopted a new homesite they tend to return each spring after enjoying their winter in Brazil. With a martin colony, some praying mantis and a few hundred ladybirds a garden should be virtually insect-free. But that does not eliminate the fungus diseases. If all chemical sprays are denied then the gardener may be in for a big disappointment and certainly a great deal more work.

ROSES UNDER LIGHTS

Because many people have experienced success in growing certain plants under artificial light the question occasionally arises—do roses respond to fluorescent light? In a practical sense, they do not. First of all roses are not photoperiod responders. That is, they are not affected by the length or shortness of the light period, as for instance, chrysanthemums are. Secondly, according to Professor Boodley of Cornell University, the amount of light energy required to achieve any response would be at least 3,000 foot candles. This is out of the question for a homeowner and uneconomical for commercial growers. The experience of commercial rose growers who force potted roses into bloom for the Spring flower shows provides a good illustration. The plants are set out in the greenhouse in December in order to produce flowers for the first week of March. If the season is unusually bleak the lack of sun poses a serious problem, one which artificial light cannot solve. The only solution is a complicated procedure in which a skilled grower periodically drenches the plants with mist and increases the greenhouse temperature. The results are not nearly as satisfactory as they are when nature cooperates and provides sufficient sunlight.

WINTER CARE FOR COLD AREAS

In November rake up and burn all leaves between plants to prevent the wintering over and spreading of disease spores. Further protection can be provided by spraying the ground and stems at this time. Cold areas are Zones 2, 3, 4 and 5.

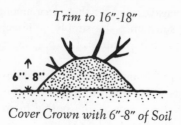

Trim to 16"-18"

6"- 8"

Cover Crown with 6"-8" of Soil

Drawing 11.

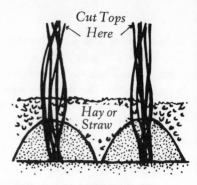

Cut Tops
Here

Hay or
Straw

Drawing 12.

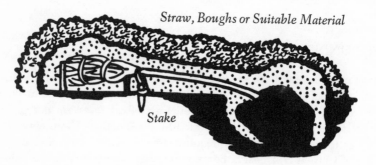

Straw, Boughs or Suitable Material

Stake

Drawing 13.

HYBRID TEAS AND FLORIBUNDAS: Prior to the first heavy frost hill up hybrid tea and floribunda roses with 6 to 8 inches of soil. After the ground is frozen cover the mounded plants with straw, salt hay or evergreen boughs for protection against sub-zero temperatures.

CLIMBERS: Truss climbers securely to trellis or supports to avoid winter damage from wind whip.

TREE ROSES: After the first light frost dig up tree roses, lay them in a trench and cover completely with soil. They will be in fine shape when spring comes around and you uncover and replant them.

SPECIES ROSE LIST

Rosa alba Incarnata: double white flowers up to 2 inches across, large orange to scarlet fruits; has been used since Colonial days. Zone 4.

Rosa amblyotis: red single flowers 2 inches across; known as the Kamchatka rose, it is hardy in Zone 2.

Rosa californica: single pink flowers 1½ inches across borne in clusters; mainly valuable to its native West Coast area.

Rosa carolina: small, single red flowers and brightly colored red fruits; native to the Eastern United States from Maine to Texas. Zone 4.

Rosa centifolia: pink flowers that are 2½ inches across and very fragrant; known as the Cabbage rose, has been popular for centuries. Zone 5.

Rosa centifolia muscosa: double flowers that have sepals and pedicels covered with mosslike growth for which it has been named the Moss rose. Zone 5.

Rosa coriifolia Froebelii: creamy-white flowers 2½ inches across that are produced profusely; has bright red fruits. Known as the Froebel rose. Zone 4.

Rosa damascena: large clusters of pale pink to red flowers 2½ inches across; very fragrant. Known as the Damask rose, it is thought to have been grown in England by the early Romans. Zone 4.

Rosa damascena versicolor: partially double flowers are white-striped and blotched with pink. This is the historic York and Lancaster rose. Zone 4.

Rosa Eglanteria: single pink flowers and attractive orange to scarlet fruits; foliage is sweet scented. Known as the Sweetbrier, it is found in Europe in hedgerows. Zone 4.

Rosa foetida: single flowers are 2 to 3 inches across and a deep yellow—the name arises from their unpleasant odor. Has been popular, along with its varieties, for four centuries. Zone 4.

Rosa foetida bicolor: single, coppery-red flowers; known as the Austrian Copper Brier. Zone 4.

Rosa foetida persiana: double flowers are yellow; known as the Persian Yellow rose. Zone 4.

Rosa gallica: brick-red single flowers are 2½ inches across. Known as the French rose. Zone 5.

Rosa gallica Officinalis: double pink to red flowers; long known as the Apothecary rose. Zone 5.

Rosa Harisonii: a hybrid resulting from a cross between *Rosa foetida* and *Rosa spinosissima*, it has outstanding double-yellow, 2-inch flowers. Zone 4.

Rosa Hugonis: single, canary-yellow flowers, 2 inches across; early flowering. Zone 5.

Rosa laevigata: single white flowers are 3 inches across and highly fragrant; very popular in the South. Zone 7.

Rosa multiflora: small white single flowers and small bright red fruits. Widely recommended as a "living hedge," it is useful only on farm land where space is no object because it tends to spread 12 to 15 feet wide and once established, it is difficult to eliminate. Ideal haven for wild life and good as a cattle barrier but if your plot is of average size, avoid it at all costs. Zone 5.

Rosa nitida: single rosy-red flowers, 2 inches across, small fruits; glossy foliage that turns bright red in fall. Zone 3.

Rosa nutkana: pink flowers, 2½ inches across. Hardy in Alaska. Zone 2.

Rosa odorata: double pink flowers, 2½ inches across; frequently evergreen in the South. Long cultivated in China, its common name, the tea rose, comes from the pleasant fragrance of its flowers. Zone 7.

Rose rubrifolia: single red flowers are not outstanding but plant is valuable for its hardiness and red foliage which gives rise to its common name, the Redleaf rose. Zone 2.

Rosa rugosa: varieties have both single and double flowers of red and white; fall foliage is an attractive orange. One of the most popular species, it grows well by the seashore since the plants survive salt water spray. Very hardy. Zone 2.

Rosa setigera: single rose-colored flowers 2 inches across. Known as the Prairie rose, it tends to spread and grows 12 to 15 feet tall. Zone 4.

Rosa spinosissima alba plena: white flowers are very double and 3 inches across; one of the best of the Scotch roses. Zone 4.

Rosa virginiana: single pink flowers; bright red fruits; foliage an attractive red and orange in fall. Known as the Virginia rose, it is very popular and easily pruned to a height of 3 feet. Zone 3.

Rosa Wichuraiana: small white flowers do not appear until late summer; glossy green foliage is semi-evergreen; vigorous growing, it is the only truly trailing rose and is valuable as a ground cover. Known as the Memorial rose. Zone 5.

HOW TO USE THE PLANT HARDINESS ZONE MAP

This map shows the expected minimum temperatures in ten zones, each of which varies by ten degrees from its adjoining zone.

Once you find which zone your home is in it will not only indicate minimum temperatures for your area but will also aid you in using the *Twenty Step Rose Care Calendar* which is divided according to zones 3 to 10. These include all of the United States.

Again it must be emphasized that the map may not be accurate for a specific area. There are climate islands in which temperatures may be lower or higher than average. For instance, temperatures in the author's home town, Ho-Ho-Kus, New Jersey, average ten degrees lower, winter and summer, than those reported daily for New York City which is little more than twenty miles away. By comparing daily temperatures with those listed in your local newspaper you should be able to determine whether or not your area conforms with the average.

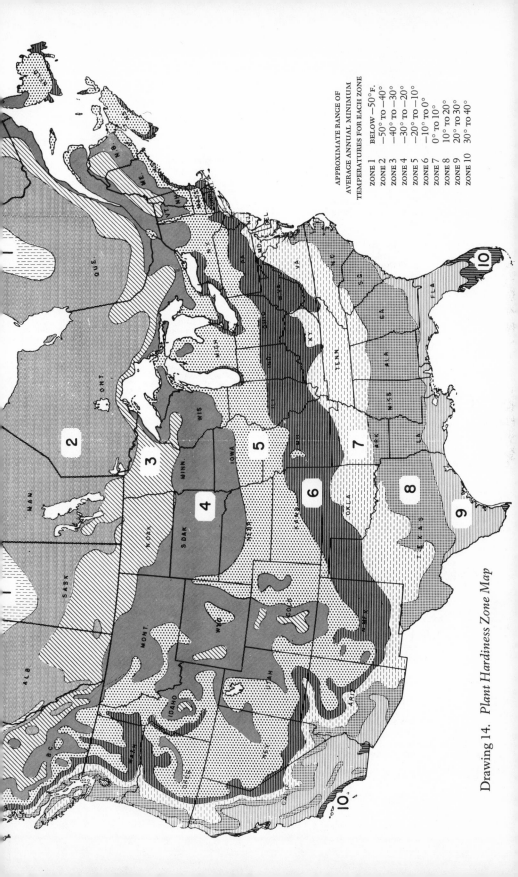

Drawing 14. *Plant Hardiness Zone Map*

THE TWENTY STEP
ROSE CALENDAR*

	ZONES 3-4	ZONE 5
EARLY SEASON		
1. Remove winter protection.	After frosts end	Same
2. Prune established plants. Remove winterkill; shape Hybrid Teas & Floribundas; not Climbers.	Before planting bare-root roses	Same
3. Plant bare-root roses, following instructions closely.	April-May	April
4. Remove soil mound on newly planted roses as new growth appears.	May	Apr.-May
5. Fertilize.	When old plants show 1-inch new growth	Same
6. Mulch beds.	After feeding	Same
7. Water weekly.	When less than 1-inch of rain fall	Same
8. Spray or dust.	Weekly after first buds break or within 24 hrs. of rainfall	Same
9. Weed. If no mulch, weed beds by shallow cultivation.	Late May	May
MIDSEASON		
10. Plant potted roses.	June on	Late May on
11. Fertilize after first peak bloom is reached.	Late June	Mid June
12. Prune.	Spent flowers	Same
13. Spray or dust.	Weekly, but not when temperature exceeds 80°F.	Same
14. Water.	Weekly when less than 1-inch of rainfall	Same
LATE SEASON		
15. Fertilize—last feeding.	July	Late July
16. Spray or dust.	Weekly till frost	Same
17. Plant bare-root rose.	Spring only	Spring only
18. Prune old wood Climbers.	Early October	Mid Oct.
19. Winter protection; hill up Hybrid Teas & Floribundas to 8 inches; truss Climbers; bury Tree roses.	Late October	Early Nov.
20. Order rose catalogs.	Indulge yourself in armchair gardening.	Same

*Based on plant Zone Hardiness Map of U.S. Department of Agriculture.

ZONE 6	ZONE 7	ZONE 8	ZONES 9-10
Same	Same	None	None
Same	Same	Same	Dec.-Jan.
Mar.-Apr.	Feb.-Mar.	Jan.-Feb.	Dec.-Feb.
Mid Apr.-Early May	Mar.-Apr.	Feb.-Mar.	Jan.-Feb.
Same	Same	Same	Same
Same	Same	Same	Same
Same	Same	Same	Same
Same	Same	Same	Same
Late Apr.	Apr.	Mar.	Feb.-Mar.
Mid May on	Early May on	Early Apr. on	Late Mar. on
Early June	Late May	Mid May	Early May
Same	Same	Same	Same
Same	Same	Same	Same
Same	Same	Same	Same
Early Aug.	Mid Aug.	Sept.	Oct.
Same	Same	Same	Same
Nov.	Oct.	None	None
Late Oct.	Early Nov.	Mid Nov.	Late Nov.
Mid Nov.	Late Nov.	None	None
Same	Same	Same	Same

6

ROSE CULTURE
FOR SPECIAL AREAS

I sometimes think that never blows so red
The Rose as where some buried Caesar bled
OMAR KHAYYAM
1070-1123
(EDWARD FITZGERALD TRANSLATION)

R oses can be grown successfully in many difficult soils and climates by any gardener willing to go to some trouble. The advice which follows gives all necessary details.

SOUTH OF THE MASON-DIXON LINE

This covers a large area and a considerable climatic spread. Annual rainfall throughout most of the South averages 40 to 60 inches, with average annual temperatures ranging from 50 to 60 degrees F. in the northernmost areas to 70 degrees in lower Florida. Temperatures in summer go above 100 degrees but in the winter the thermometer can go below zero even in the Middle South. On the Plant Hardiness Zone Map this area would include zones 8, 9 and 10.

Bare-root roses can be planted from December through February. Rose culture will vary according to the three basic types of soil and average rainfall. Raised beds are used to provide drainage and protect plants in areas of excessive moisture.

Sandy soil in this region is frequently infected with nematodes and must be fumigated before planting roses. Leaching, or the washing away of chemical elements, is so rapid that frequent and heavy feeding is required—with minor elements added since most of the minerals are lacking. While peat moss is a necessity the ideal soil preparation would include a mixture of peat moss composted with cow manure and sludge. The graft union should be an inch above ground— which necessitates a continuous check for suckers from the rootstock. Mulches help retain moisture and where salt is a problem, pulverized gypsum, mixed thoroughly into the soil, will help control salinity. Afternoon shade is helpful but early morning sun is important to dry off the dew quickly. Too severe cutting of plants will deprive them of necessary foliage and weaken them dangerously. Especially in the first year pruning should be restricted to thinning out and shaping plants. When blooms are cut, be satisfied with moderate stems and leave as much foliage as possible.

Where soil is very heavy, that is along the Gulf of Mexico from New Orleans to Texas, organic material must be added and the bed levels raised about 2 feet. The graft union should still be kept an inch above the soil level but the roots can be encouraged to spread outward rather than downward because of the water level and drainage. A 2- to 3-inch mulch is necessary. Where the soil is sandy-clay, roses will do well with normal culture. In no case is any form of winter protection needed. While mildew is no threat, protective measures should be taken against blackspot and insects.

ARID REGIONS

Roses can be grown successfully even when the temperature reaches 120 degrees as proved in Arizona. Humus is needed where the soil is sandy. Where it is heavy, sand should be added. If drainage is a problem a 6-inch layer of gravel or tile shards at the bottom of the hole will alleviate the condition. In most cases the soil will be alkaline so avoid the use of lime, bone meal or ashes all of which are alkaline. The addition of sulphur will not only correct alkalinity but also add iron and magnesium. Fertilizer should not be used in planting; in fact, it cannot be used safely until the plant is well established. From then on feeding should be on a once a month schedule because of the rapid growth in this climate. Bare-root bushes can be planted in January and February with the graft union kept about an inch above ground level. Watering is best handled by giving the beds a heavy flooding twice a week during spring, summer and fall and once a week in winter. A 3- to 4-inch retaining curb around the beds will hold all the water where it belongs. At each watering fill the bed level with the top of the curb to ensure enough for deep soaking. A regular pest and disease program is required but spray or dust should be avoided during the day if temperatures exceed 80 degrees F.

ALASKA

Louise Marx who lives at Anchorage and writes for the *Anchorage Daily Times* has been very successful with her roses. In fact she finds the combination of temperate days and the midnight sun that shines most of the night during early and mid-September results in some exceptionally beautiful flowers. Though some people in Alaska plan on replacing their roses each year, Mrs. Marx has found a way to carry hers through the winter without the backbreaking task of burying them. After the ground is frozen she piles sawdust around the plants, ties the canes together and then wraps them with heavyweight metal foil, leaving the top open for ventilation. This protects the roots during the spring freeze-and-thaw period. After frost danger is over she removes the protection and cuts the canes back to green wood and enjoys flowers through summer until September. Natural peat moss is available in this area and is added to the topsoil. In the bottom 12 inches of the hole is a mixture of equal parts of compost and peat moss followed with about 6 inches of an equal mixture of sand and loam. The graft union is planted two inches below the soil level. Mrs. Marx adds 2 cupfuls of bonemeal to each plant, and because organic matter is lacking she makes a liquid fertilizer which she applies to the soil around each plant twice a month during June, July and the first two weeks in August.

Spraying is necessary even in Alaska, although Mrs. Marx imports ladybirds to combat the aphids. She releases them at regular intervals since they tend to fly off after their first heavy feeding. Although wind is a problem she overcame it by using a growth of spruce trees as her windbreak.

HAWAII

Since everything grows so luxuriantly in Hawaii roses have considerable competition from the native plants that require little or no care. Also, some Hawaiian nurserymen advise the practice followed in greenhouses where roses grow the year round—replace them every 3 to 5 years. However, rose plants have been known to grow at least 10 years and no doubt could continue much longer with proper care. Because of the volcanic composition of the soil a fertilizer containing potash or phosphate must be worked down below the surface and a heavy watering must follow each monthly feeding. As in other warm areas the graft union is placed an inch above ground level. During dry periods plants should be watered twice a week. Blackspot is not a serious problem but mildew and insects must be guarded against and a weekly spray program must be conducted the whole year round since there is no dormant season.

SEASHORE GARDENS

It is quite possible to grow roses within 200 to 300 feet of the ocean provided certain precautions are taken. The basic problems to be considered are salt, sandy soil and wind. Since more damage results from the dehydration caused by constant winds than from salt or sand the first consideration is a windbreak. This may be a low wall or plantings of Japanese black pine, black plum, American holly or other plants that seem to thrive on salt and sand. The rugosa roses, both the species and *R. rugosa alba*, naturalize themselves on the beach and some of the old ramblers also do very well.

Since modern roses will not grow in sand alone it is necessary to add organic matter. Peat moss, leaf mold, manure, compost and where possible, topsoil, will serve the purpose. No fertilizer should be used at planting time but anticipate heavy leaching out of foods from the soil and prepare to feed small amounts often during the growing season. Obviously drainage is no problem but all roses should be well watered once a week. It does no harm to wash salt off the leaves provided this is done while there is plenty of sunlight to dry them off quickly.

One seaside rosarian found his best answer to the soil problem was to plant his roses in good soil in peach baskets which, after growth was well started, were transported to the site and dropped into holes with soil tamped in around the edges. By the time the baskets disintegrated the plants were well established.

Weekly spraying is necessary but because of the cool nights along the shore plus above average moisture conditions, roses produce a great many blooms that are more intense in color than elsewhere. The deep vivid coloring is quite startling and is a strong incentive to establish a seashore rose garden.

NORTHERN NEW ENGLAND

An excellent paper, "Winter Protection of Hybrid Roses," was prepared for Vermont rose growers by Harrison L. Flint, Ornamental Horticulturist for the University of Vermont. It is presented here in its entirety. The techniques outlined are applicable in all areas having comparable winter temperatures.

"Rose plants can be killed or injured during winter in any of several different ways. These include:

1. Direct injury to tops or roots from extreme cold.
2. Root injury from drying-out as a result of plants being heaved out of the ground by alternate freezing and thawing.
3. Rapid variation in temperature caused by warming of stems by strong winter sunshine and then rapid freezing.
4. Injury caused by animals.
5. Snow or ice breakage.

"Injury from extreme cold can be avoided only by selecting the most hardy varieties. Even some of the 'sub-zero' varieties offered for sale have failed to overwinter well in our area. Most varieties have not been thoroughly tested for winter hardiness, so Vermont rose gardeners must be willing to experiment for themselves. Once we have selected a reasonably hardy variety, there are a few simple precautions that we can take to increase the chances of survival.

"*Mulches.* A mulch of several inches of insulating material will help to stabilize the soil temperature. Also, soil temperatures will remain higher than they would without this protective cover.

"Snow, one of the best mulches, unfortunately cannot always be depended upon. So other mulching materials must be used. Some good ones are peat moss, clean straw, buckwheat hulls, rock or glass wool insulation, cut evergreen branches, cornstalks, ground corncobs, marsh hay, wood chips, or any other material that will settle lightly on the soil surface without excessive packing, cause no toxic effects, and be reasonably attractive and inexpensive.

"*Mounding.*   A 2- to 4-inch layer of mulch usually is not enough in our winters. Many gardeners have obtained good results by mounding mulching material or soil around the plants to a height of a foot or more. When doing this it is important to use a porous material. Too often a dense soil mound cuts off the oxygen supply to the roots and the plants succumb to the treatment rather than to the winter.

"Before mulching or mounding, the fall cleanup should be completed, removing all plant debris and diseased parts. Even with these treatments, tip dieback can be expected. This is not usually serious, as the canes will be pruned back at least to 18 inches next spring and the injured tips will be removed at that time."

7
A ROSE IS BORN

This is an art which does mend nature, change it rather; but the art itself is nature.
H. B. Ellwanger
1882

The eternal search for new roses is unquestionably one of the most powerful lures inherent in the "Queen of Flowers."

The early botanist who scoured the world looking for new species, the scientist who continually develops new varieties, the home gardener who rips out an old favorite to make room for the latest introduction—each has his eye on the end of a rainbow. But when he finds it, perfection is not enough and the search continues.

The latest edition of *Modern Roses*, published jointly by the McFarland Company and the American Rose Society, lists all known roses. Among them are 9,410 varieties and 338 species roses. In addition, 781 names are identified as synonyms and variations. Though most of the varieties were developed by professional hybridists a representative group are the work of amateurs. Because of the returns, monetary and otherwise, this practice is likely to continue despite the tremendous odds against success—odds which favor the commercial hybridist with extensive growing facilities and ample financial backing.

Other than protection of his property there is no reason why an amateur should patent his new rose. And if he wishes to name it for someone very special there is no reason why he should register the name unless he feels the rose warrants such action.

One of the most flattering honors is to have one's name given to a new rose. At the same time, it would be difficult to imagine a more satisfying accomplishment than success in working with nature to develop an infinitely beautiful rose that never existed before. Furthermore, a worthwhile new rose can become a valuable property besides ensuring the originator a permanent place in the International Rose Register. The standard royalties in America are 15 percent of the retail price for the first and second year after introduction, 10 percent for the third year and 5 percent thereafter.

52. *When a new rose is developed and a patent applied for, two paintings must be submitted to the Government showing the cane foliage and various phases of the flower.*

For instance, an amateur hybridist, William Zombory of Detroit, Michigan, developed two climbers which were introduced commercially as Coral Satin and Coralita and were priced at $3.00 each. He assigned them to the Jackson & Perkins Company which obtained the patents and also licensed other firms to grow them. Every plant sold brings Mr. Zombory a royalty.

Another amateur, Professor G. L. Jordan, formerly of the University of Illinois, hybridized the red hybrid tea rose known to many American home gardeners as Mardi Gras. During the seventeen years of patent protection the rose continues to pay dividends to the now-retired professor.

A million dollars is a conservative estimate of the earnings through sales and royalties of the hothouse rose, Better Times. One of nature's gifts, it is a sport of Briarcliff. For many years after its 1934 introduction by the J. H. Hill Co., this variety was a favorite of commercial cut flower growers. Until recently it was usually the rose provided anyone who walked into a florist shop and asked for "a dozen red roses."

PLANT PATENT REQUIREMENTS

What are the requirements for claiming a new rose variety? The U.S. Plant Patent Act of 1930, which grants the owner the right to prohibit others from asexually reproducing a patented plant or selling it for seventeen years, provides these requisites.

New and distinct varieties of roses may be:

Hybrids, resulting from cross-pollinization of two species, two varieties or a species and a variety;

Sports, arising from bud variation;

Mutants, seedling variants created by self pollinization of species.

Among the characteristics that may distinguish a new variety are: habit of growth; immunity to disease; resistance to cold, drought, heat, wind or soil condition; color of leaf, flower, fruit or stems; fragrance; productivity, including continuous blooming; form and ease of asexual reproduction. The latter includes reproduction by grafting, budding or cuttings. Excluded is propagation from seeds which is a sexual process. Since species roses reproduce true to form from seeds, they cannot be patented.

PATENT COSTS   The government does not grant patents indiscriminately. Excluding the time involved, costs involved in a patent average $500. These include: two duplicate paintings showing the plant in various stages, $100; initial preparation and filing of U.S. Plant Patent Application, $275; government filing fee, $30; preparation and recording assignment, $20; final government fee, $40.

HOW TO DEVELOP A NEW ROSE

How should you proceed, then, if you want to produce a new rose which you alone can name and control during the seventeen years of its patent life?

Both sports and mutants are produced by nature. But you must have the ability to recognize them and the know-how to propagate the new varieties for enough years to be certain that distinguishing characteristics will continue from one generation to another.

It is not uncommon to see flowers that vary from the others on the same plant. Sometimes these arise from suckers that grow from the original wild or species plant on which the named rose was grafted. These are worthless. But if one stem produces distinctly different flowers they can be propagated by taking budding eyes from the stem and grafting them near the base of a wild plant, such as R. *multiflora*. Once the grafted eye has produced about six inches of new growth remove the remaining stem of the wild plant just above the graft. Then all the vigor of the root system will be channeled into the budded section. You are now on your way toward learning whether the new flowers are truly different, worthwhile and will remain constant through successive periods of propagation.

This was the process used by the J. H. Hill Company to establish Better Times as a new and superior variety distinctly different from its parent, Briarcliff.

The majority of new roses are produced through hybridization, that is, the cross-pollinization of two parent roses. Odds against success in this process are the fly in the ointment. They are conservatively estimated at about 10,000 to 1.

By far the largest rose research operation in the world is conducted by the Jackson & Perkins Company. Directed by E. S. Boerner, Treasurer and Director of Plant Research for the firm, it comprises an East Coast operation in a series of greenhouses and test fields at their Newark, New York, headquarters, and an outdoor research program covering some 100 acres handled by William A. Warriner at Pleasanton, California. In addition, the firm imports the best varieties developed by the top hybridists in Europe. New varieties from abroad

53.   *The first step in hybridization is to collect pollen from the stamens which surround the pistils. The bloom is selected just before the petals begin to open. The petals are first cut away to expose the stamens which are then placed in airtight boxes.*

are given thorough tests under the widely varying climatic conditions in the United States before they are judged worthy of introduction. The cost of the entire operation is more than $300,000 a year.

The two research operations produce more than 200,000 seedlings a year. Of these, not more than five or six are expected to be worthy of commercial distribution. The interval between the initial hybridization and formal introduction of a new variety may range between seven and ten years. This is why it is estimated by commercial rose hybridists that the development of a new rose costs a minimum of $50,000.

Sometimes nature favors the hybridist. For instance, Boerner produced two of today's greatest roses, Fashion and Vogue, from seeds in the same pod. The odds against this are even greater than they are for the amateur to come up with a really good new rose.

TECHNIQUES OF HYBRIDIZATION

The techniques of producing a new rose are the same for professional and amateur. Consider first a quality that will make your new creation outstanding. Whether it is to be fragrance, color, size or shape of bloom, or a plant that will do well in your climate, be it cold, hot or temperate, settle on an objective. Then study your parent plants to determine the best way to achieve your goal. If you want fragrance, work with two highly fragrant parent roses. Even then

54, 55.   *If fertilization takes place a rose hip is produced. Inside the rose hip are seeds.*

you may not be successful because modern roses are so inbred that you cannot expect returns on the basis of the Mendelian laws. If you are not familiar with Mendelian theory you should study it in a basic botany text.

Choose your parent roses on the basis of your objective; then develop patience. It will stand you in good stead should nature not choose to provide you with a bonanza.

A knowledge of the anatomy of the rose is necessary to an understanding of the process of hybridization. First of all, roses are bisexual, there are both male and female parts in the center of each flower. In nature the male part, the stamen, fertilizes the female part, the pistil. Or the wind or an insect can bring foreign pollen which may fertilize the female part.

To hybridize a rose artificially you must select pollen from the male parent, bring this to the female parent and prevent nature from interfering at any stage. To prepare the female parent it is necessary to remove the male parts, the pollen-bearing stamens that form a ring around the female pistils in the center of each flower. This should be done in the early morning before the blossom opens. Select a bud that is ready to open and remove all the petals with a pair of ordinary bathroom tweezers. Then carefully pluck off the stamens. The pistils will not be ready to receive pollen until they are ripe and ooze the sticky substance that is used by the plant to capture pollen. This should be toward evening of the same day or perhaps within a day or two. While waiting, cover the emasculated flower with a small cellophane bag to prevent contamination by insects or wind-borne pollen.

Meanwhile you should have gathered pollen from the male parent. Use the same process as above except that when you remove the stamens store them in a small box. Place the box in a warm room away from sun and wind. When the stamens are dry the golden pollen grains may be shaken free. Remove the cellophane bag from the female parent and apply pollen to the pistils with either a clean camel's hair brush or a fuzzy pipe cleaner. Again, protect the "bride" with the cellophane bag.

The pollen should then slip down the tubes of the pistils into the ovary at the bottom. If fertilization is successful a seed-bearing rose "hip" or "apple" will form in late summer or early fall. Inside the pod are the seeds you seek. Remove and drop them into a glass of water. Discard any that float. Plant the others a quarter inch deep in a flat containing good loamy soil. At this stage you will need a greenhouse even if it is only a window-box type, exposed to full sunlight. Keep the soil in the flats moist but not soaked. If planting is done in October small shoots should appear between December and March.

SEEDLINGS   When a seedling has produced three sets of leaves transplant it into a 2-inch pot. By the time it is 4 to 5 inches high the first bloom will appear. This is an exciting moment, but don't uncork the champagne yet. The first flower, which is not always representative, may be disappointing. The only way

56. *The seeds are planted and labelled in a flat. When they sprout, the tiny plants are replanted in small individual pots.*

Drawing 15. *Before you hybridize, study the parentage of roses. The lineage of roses Polynesian Sunset and John F. Kennedy can be traced back more than a century. In some cases (shown in shaded area in the center) the two totally different roses had common parents.*

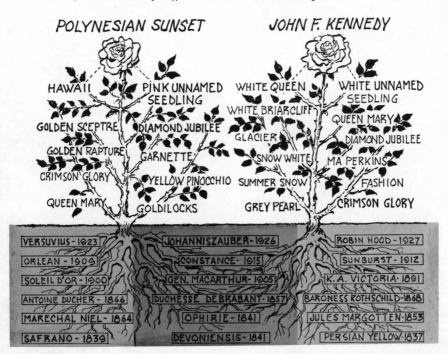

POLYNESIAN SUNSET   JOHN F. KENNEDY

HAWAII   PINK UNNAMED   WHITE QUEEN   WHITE UNNAMED
                 SEEDLING   SEEDLING
                           WHITE BRIARCLIFF   QUEEN MARY
GOLDEN SCEPTRE   DIAMOND JUBILEE   DIAMOND JUBILEE
                           GLACIER
GOLDEN RAPTURE   GARNETTE   MA PERKINS
                           SNOW WHITE
CRIMSON GLORY   YELLOW PINOCCHIO SUMMER SNOW   FASHION
QUEEN MARY   GOLDILOCKS   GREY PEARL   CRIMSON GLORY

VERSUVIUS - 1923   JOHANNISZAUBER - 1926   ROBIN HOOD - 1927
ORLEAN - 1909   CONSTANCE - 1915   SUNBURST - 1912
SOLEIL D'OR - 1900   GEN. MACARTHUR - 1905   K. A. VICTORIA - 1891
ANTOINE DUCHER - 1866 DUCHESSE DE BRABANT - 1857 BARONESS ROTHSCHILD - 1868
MARECHAL NIEL - 1864   OPHIRIE - 1841   JULES MARGOTTEN - 1853
SAFRANO - 1839   DEVONIENSIS - 1841   PERSIAN YELLOW - 1837

to reach a decision is to allow the plant to mature fully. The normal process in the garden takes three years but professionals speed it up a year or more by grafting budding eyes onto established plants, as described below in Rose Production.

Though most garden roses can be used in hybridization some are more productive than others, hence the need to understand something of their background. For instance, the new red hybrid tea rose, Hallmark, a cross between Chrysler Imperial and Independence, has a family tree that can be traced all the way back to 1590 to the Austrian Copper Rose.

Since the Hallmark has such a distinguished background the chances are that it should make an excellent parent. If you wish to produce a red rose,

57. *(Left) Wild stock is planted in the fields a year before budding begins. A special tool is used to insure that all the cuttings will be planted to a uniform depth. They are planted in holes in a strip of plastic which both preserves moisture and prevents growth of weeds.*

58. *(Right) To produce new hybrids in large quantities, they must be grafted onto wild plants that have already been growing for a year. This process is handled by two-man teams: a budder followed by a winder.*

select a second red rose for the other parent. If you want a new color, choose a yellow or pink variety for the second parent. In any case, you should have a definite objective.

ROSE PRODUCTION

When the hybridizing and testing have been completed and a rose is ready for public introduction there remains the problem of producing it in large enough quantities for distribution throughout the country. The original plant is the source of all future bushes of that particular variety. Fortunately the testing period requires a considerable number of plants, ensuring a reasonable source of budding wood. The stems of each plant have several dormant "eyes" or buds which can be found on canes where there are sets of 5 leaflet leaves.

The production cycle has three phases: growing the understock, producing the budwood and, finally, making the desired hybrid plant.

At the world's largest rose ranch, the Jackson & Perkins 6,500-acre operation near Phoenix, Arizona, the procedure is as follows.

GROWING THE UNDERSTOCK   In November crews go into the fields and cut long canes called "whips" from the wild roses that will be used for understock. Depending on how the final plants are to be used these may include Manetti, Dr. Huey (commonly called Shafter), Odorata or Burr Multiflora roses.

The whips are tied into bundles of 200 to 250, and then cut into 9-inch lengths. From each of these "cutting sticks" all but the top two or three buds are removed to prevent the stock from suckering after it has been budded. Suckering occurs when stems grow from the wild rose plant below the graft union. If they continue to grow they will convert the plant back to its wild state. The bottom of each cutting stick is cut on a slant so soil will not pack the cell walls when it is shoved into the ground in the field.

A special tractor lays down a strip of black mulch paper to keep soil moisture in and to control weeds. At the same time it punches holes eight inches apart. Beginning in January the cuttings are planted in these holes by hand. Each cutting is slipped into a special metal sleeve which prevents the worker from planting it upside-down and also ensures that a standard 3 inches is pushed below the soil line.

After the cuttings have been planted, water is channeled into the fields. As it soaks below ground level it seals off the slanted end of the cutting so that air cannot pass down the stem and dry it out. By the following spring these cuttings have rooted and have produced healthy vigorous plants ready for the budding operation that will change them into the desired hybrid variety.

PRODUCTION OF BUDWOOD   Meanwhile, the second stage of the operation requires the production of budding wood of the desired varieties. If the rose

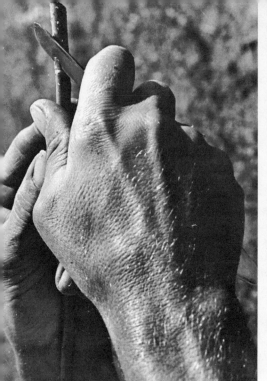

59, 60, 61.   (Above, left) The budder shaves a budding eye, plus a small amount of the bark off a cutting. (Right) He pushes aside bark so that the budding eye can be slipped inside. (Left) Then the second man in the team, the winder, wraps tape around the operation.

62, 63.   (Opposite, left) The tape is placed carefully so that the budding eye is exposed and can grow out after the wound heals. By this time the tape will have rotted and fallen away. (Opposite, right) After the stem grows out from the graft, the top of the wild plant is cut off so that all the strength from the roots goes into the grafted hybrid. The plant is grown for a year during which time the new cane is pruned so that three or four new canes will branch out making a full plant which will produce only the desired hybrid flowers.

happens to be a new introduction the growing cycle will stretch over a four-year period to produce the quarter million budding eyes needed. A single plant will provide enough eyes to make 10 other plants in the first year, and in the next these 10 will make from 10 to 20 plants each. In succeeding years they may be counted on to produce from 40 to 50 budding eyes as the plants mature and grow larger.

Budwood is harvested in the fall from well-matured branches cut from the rose varieties that are to be propagated. It is cut into 10- to 12-inch lengths, wrapped in wet burlap and placed in a pre-cooling room where a crew of women, called scion cleaners, remove the thorns and foliage.

After cleaning the budwood, the women dip it in fungicide and prepare it for storage. It is wrapped in two sheets of wet newspaper, then two sheets of dry newspaper with a final plastic wrapping to prevent it from drying out. Labeled as to variety, count and date of processing, the bundles are stored in wooden boxes in a refrigeration room at 28 degrees to 30 degrees F. This temperature lightly freezes the packages and holds the buds dormant until budding time in spring.

MAKING THE HYBRID PLANT   Beginning in March two-man teams—a budder and a winder—go into the fields which by this time are seemingly endless rows of vigorously growing wild roses. Just above the ground level the budder wipes the cane clean and with a special knife makes a vertical cut in the bark and then a short horizontal cut at the top to form a T. He then folds back the two edges of bark and inserts a bud or "eye" which he has neatly sliced from the budwood. Buds must be removed very precisely so that their growing surface can come into close contact with the growing surface of the wild plant. It takes a man at least three years to become proficient in this delicate operation. Experts can make as many as 3,000 buddings a day, their fingers moving faster than the eye can follow.

When the budder has finished inserting the eye and replacing the bark, the winder wraps a strip of special rubber around the bark so that the "eye" is left exposed and free to grow outward while the bark is held firmly in place. By the time the bud begins to unite with the wild rose cane the rubber bandage has rotted and fallen away.

Within a few months the bud grows into a sturdy new stem. The crews go back into the fields, cut halfway through the top growth of the wild plant about an inch above the bud and bend the cut portion over toward the budded stem so that sap will be forced into it. To cut off the unwanted growth in one operation could be too drastic and would weaken the plant. Not until the following spring is the top growth removed completely. By then the new stem is healthily utilizing all the sap from the vigorous root system of the wild rose. It also is pruned at the top to encourage the production of side shoots. During the rest of the season the plants are watered, fertilized and regularly sprayed so that by fall they are ready for harvesting.

HARVESTING   Digging starts in October. Since the weather in Arizona still encourages growth, the water supply is cut off prior to digging in order to force the plants into dormancy. Afterwards a mowing machine cuts the bushes down to a uniform height. They are stripped of their foliage either mechanically or by sheep. The animals love the leaves and are not bothered by the thorns, nor do they injure the plants while browsing.

The plants are dug by a special U-shaped digger drawn by a tractor and are then graded, bundled and carefully packed into freight cars. From Arizona they are sent to the Jackson & Perkins headquarters at Newark, New York. Whereas temperatures are still high in Arizona there is a strong likelihood of freezing temperatures in the North. Therefore ice is put in one end of the car for the warm part of the trip and an automatic heater at the other end is set to operate when outside temperatures approach the freezing level.

On arrival in upstate New York the plants are moistened again and stored in refrigerated rooms at a constant temperature of 34 degrees F. until time to ship them out to home gardeners.

8

A ROSE IS A BOUQUET

And take each blossom, rich and rare,
Which thou may'st find in beauty there;
Combine their color, form, and grace.
                    S. B. Parsons
                    1847

A small but vocal faction of gardeners urges that roses be left in their natural state in the garden, but most people prefer to enjoy their blooms twice, in the garden and in the house.

Considerable research has been conducted into methods of increasing the life of cut roses in vases. By using laboratory-tested methods you can add several days to the enjoyment of a bouquet of roses. This is especially important in the winter when your supply of cut roses comes from a florist, unless you live in the Deep South.

Incidentally, the average cost of a dozen hybrid tea roses from the florist is between $10 and $12—and well worth it! While garden varieties vary in the quantity of blooms they produce, you should expect at least three to four dozen flowers from a plant during a normal season. (With some varieties you can either add to or multiply this figure!) This means that your original investment of about $3.50 has returned flowers worth a minimum of $30 to $40. With this in mind it is even more essential to treat roses properly for maximum enjoyment.

HOW TO CUT FLOWERS

It is interesting to note that cutting flowers from prolific bloomers serves to increase production, ensuring a constant succession. In all cases temper your enthusiasm according to the needs of the plant. Do not cut so many flowers that the plant no longer has sufficient leaves to produce the necessary food to remain healthy and able to bloom again.

Also, when cutting a stem, be sure to leave at least two sets of five leaflet leaves. The new flower will come from the axil (the upper angle between the top leaflet and the stem) so choose one that faces away from the center of the plant,

117

preventing branches from crossing in the middle. Use a very sharp knife and cut at a slant a quarter inch above the top leaflet. The reason for this is as follows: Water is the element that makes flowers stand up proudly and keeps the petals firm or "turgid." When a stem is cut its supply of water must be replaced. If the stem is cut straight across and placed in a container of water it may rest on the bottom of the container and impede the passage of water up to the flower. Since the petals of a flower are constantly losing water through evaporation it won't be long before they become limp and change color. Therefore make a long slanting cut and place the stem in water as quickly as possible.

WHEN TO CUT FLOWERS

Cut roses late in the afternoon when the sugar level is at its highest or in the early morning, because the plant has been absorbing water during the night and the moisture level is at its maximum at this stage.

Water travels up the stem of a rose through a series of cells just underneath the bark. This is another reason for the slanting cut which exposes a larger cell area to the water supply for absorption. Bacteria may form in the vase water and clog up the stem cells causing the flower to wilt. To prevent this start with a clean container. If possible, change the water each day and cut a little off the base of the stems. Better still, add to the water a flower preservative, such as "Roselife" or "Floralife." Also, remove any leaves below the water line to prevent them from decaying and producing bacteria. One thing more. Forget aspirin, salt or any of the other old wives' remedies. They are totally useless.

HARDENING OFF

Commercial cut rose growers use a process called "hardening" which is equally effective for the home rose grower. Here the roses, standing in the water with preservative added, are stored under refrigeration at 34 degrees F. for 24 hours. Hardening can extend a 3- to 4-day life to almost 8 days.

Normally cold water should be used because this holds down the respiratory rate. However, if flowers are limp and not in excellent condition, hot water from the tap will increase the absorption rate and revive them faster than cold water. But it will also increase respiration, causing earlier maturation.

SUBSTANCE

The most important quality to look for when selecting roses for indoor use is *substance*. It is the thickness, firmness, texture and finish of petals and is the determining factor in the vase life of a rose.

Some strains have a crispness of petalage that automatically ensures longer life. All the Garnette family and many varieties that have Garnette blood possess

64.   Five basic steps in building a simple arrangement of a dozen blooms:
(1) Build main line with tight bud at highest point. (2) Establish
basic triangle pattern. (3) Strengthen main line, weight base and
balance center. (4) Add more open roses, facing blooms in different
directions for illusion of depth. (5) Use foliage to break the line of
the container. Three open roses complete the desired effect.

this quality. However, the Garnette flowers have flat tops rather than the high center that is most prized in the ideal "hybrid tea form."

A simple test for lasting quality is to lightly pinch the bud. It should be firm and full of petals. If it is soft the flower that will open will blast quickly. When flowers are partially open feel the petals. If they are limp the flower will not last. They should be firm and resilient if they are to last well in the vase.

ARRANGING ROSES

How you use roses indoors is a matter of taste. A single hybrid tea in a long bud vase is beautiful. A floribunda cluster will make a natural arrangement and will be long lasting. Blossoms floating in a shallow bowl require neither time nor special skills and are delightful.

65.   *Basic tools for arranging roses. In the foreground from left are twistems, lead, thin wire, clippers and scissors, and various needlepoint holders in the center. In the rear are five different containers.*

66.   *(Opposite) Steuben glassware makes an elegant container for an arrangement of the hybrid tea rose Opera.*

When it comes to the art of flower arranging, that's another matter. It is a field in which I am absolutely ignorant and since so much has been written on the subject there is no need to confuse the issue here. If you wish to learn flower arranging I would suggest that you begin with one of the many books published on the subject.*

Among the illustrations in this chapter are the winning arrangements in the Sterling Bowl Tournament, the only national flower-arranging competition. Each is accompanied by a description based on information supplied by the winner.

STERLING BOWL TOURNAMENT

Now in its eleventh year, the Sterling Bowl Tournament has become America's most important flower-arranging competition. During the first ten years 214 flower arrangers were selected for competition from a total of 600 who were nominated by state presidents of the National Council of State Garden Clubs. Each president is asked to name from one to five or more of the best flower arrangers in her state. Then a committee reviews the experience of each nominee and selects one person to represent each of the eight districts in the United States and an additional six are selected to make up a total of 14 contestants. (During the first two years all nominees were accepted—for a total of 102 contestants.)

In 1966, seven of the ten winners of the Tournament competed for the title of "the best flower arranger of the decade." The winning arrangement together with those that were judged the best for each year are shown in this chapter.

Judges for the Tournament are selected with the same care as contestants. Each must be a nationally accredited judge and recommended by state presidents who vote for the judges that are most highly regarded on a national basis.

The point system on which arrangements are judged is as follows.

Design	40
Relationship of all materials	10
Distinction	25
Originality	25
Total	100

*Hearthside Press Inc., 381 Park Avenue South, New York 1Q016, will be glad to send a descriptive list.

67. (Left) "My design was a traditional massed line. The rhythmic flow of the line was suggestive of the Hogarth curve. Gradation was achieved through the use of bud, partly open and open roses. Textural interest was gained in the luminescence of roses, the jagged edge of rose foliage, the reflective silver of the container, and the rich luster of velvet which covers the round base."

Mrs. Rolland L. Fifer, Louisville, Ky.
1956 Winner

68. (Right) "When I read your letter requesting information about the winning arrangements my first reaction was 'What did I know about what I was doing nine years ago?' Why I just arranged from my soul, or was it my heart, at that time! Well, anyway, I have taken another look at my work and it does make sense. A traditional arrangement which played up the lovely color relationship between the lavender rose and the green porcelain lining of the silver bowl. The over-all design was kept quite simple; the only foliage showing was one small side branch of rose foliage."

Mrs. C. W. Lafe, Gibsonia, Pa.
1957 Winner

69. (Left) "The design was a massed line in warm hues. Treated beech leaves were used to unite the figurine with the roses, wisteria vine repeating the movement of the arms of the figurine. The arrangement was in two parts, the upper section in an old bronze lamp base, the lower half in a cup holder. My arrangements are never planned in advance—I just work with material according to mood."

Mrs. John W. Knight, Jr. Cuyahoga Falls, Ohio
1958 Winner

70. (Right) "I let the charm of our most beautiful flower—the rose—speak for itself. There should be an abundance of bloom in every stage of its development, a pleasing blending of color, good design, a touch of compatible foliage, and no distracting accessories. I had a plywood frame made to fit the niche, with an oval cutout. I painted the frame a muted blue-green and covered the oval with silk of the same hue. I then designed the container out of sheet aluminum; the beaded trim was a rhinestone belt, painted to match the background. This subdued color brought out the brilliance and beauty of the Tanya and Golden Chalice roses."

Mrs. T. Bromley Flood, Philadelphia, Pa.
1959 Winner

71. (Left) "The name of the class was Festival of Roses. Many abstract qualities kaleidoscoped through my mind ... festival, people, happiness, motion, color, music, crescendo. The design begins with two old violins. Chalice, Golden Chalice and Mojave roses created a riotous and moving color sequence of yellow, stronger yellow touched with orange, orangey-salmon. The coppery-maroon of new foliage registered movement and motion. Gold cords used as strings further express revelry. The background fabric was grayed blue-green silk taffeta."

Mrs. John W. Minton, Roswell, New Mexico
1960 Winner

72. (Right) "A wall arrangement featuring the hybrid tea rose King's Ransom and the floribunda Peach Glow. Rose foliage is included and it repeats the green color and texture of the leather background. The container, a pewter-washed copper lavabo is mounted on a fruitwood plaque which follows the outline of the lavabo. The accessory is a pair of antique silver fighting cocks that extend the diagonal of the design to the base. For mechanics, a needlepoint holder secured by floral clay, with Oasis impaled upon it, was all that was used."

Mrs. Orrion Kattmann, Evansville, Indiana
1961 Winner

73. *(Opposite) The only arrangement by a man ever to win the Sterling Bowl Tournament rates a full page. "Carpenter had just made his phenomenal three orbits of the earth and said, 'The sky in space is velvety black.' Thus was born the title: 'The Rose Orbits in the Black Canopy of Space.'"*

Mr. John C. Dowling, Jr., Gaffney, South Carolina
1962 Winner

74. *(Left) "To create an arrangement Japanese in feeling, the container was an old Chinese bronze—early containers in ikebana were often Chinese imports and were valued possessions. As accessories I used a pair of antique Japanese incense burners, and a duck and a drake, whose necks repeated the curve of the bottle. The birds completed the asymmetrical triangle. The base was a piece of black slate."*

Mrs. R. K. Richardson, Attleboro, Mass.
1963 Winner

75. *(Right) "The American Modern style differs somewhat from modern styles in other countries. Uncluttered, simple, well organized and direct, it reflects our approach to a problem; it should have a sense of swift movement for we are an impatient mobile people. Add a bit of abstraction, or a great deal if you like, for we dare to explore the unknown, and you have all the ingredients for American Modern.*

Mrs. E. O. Barton, Houston, Texas
1964 Winner

76.   (Left) "My objective was to perfect a container that would do justice to the Rose of the Year (1965) Polynesian Sunset. A member of our Garden Club gave me permission to rummage through her "graveyard" for abandoned farm implements. My parabola curves are harrow teeth, a broken trailer hitch and an old hand iron, welded together. The holes were puttied and dried, cement was brushed on thin and left to dry for 24 hours, then painted with flat black. The bases are two oval boards, same finish. My maiden name is Goforth so I couldn't resist this description on the card in the show: 'Go Forth Into Space.'"

Mrs. Floyd Doty, Walters, Oklahoma
1965 Winner

77.   (Right) "Roses combined with a modern wood construction (natural walnut and bronze olive-green painted geometric forms, with a suspended solid walnut ball) to create a decorative accent for modern décor. The arrangement is on a black textured base, against a walnut background with a lighted panel of olive green decorator's plastic. Modern in theme, the over-all effect is one of balance, with emphasis on placement of like and unlike forms to achieve a dynamic equilibrium through balance-counter balance."

Mrs. Orrion W. Kattmann, Evansville, Indiana
1966 Winner

XXVIII. *Girl Scout is a popular floribunda with a tidy growth habit. The plant produces more blooms when its stems are cut for flower arrangements! Flowers are 3 to 3½ inches in diameter, and are golden in color.*

XXIX.   Crown Jewel is a gay floribunda with orange-red blossoms set o
by dark-green foliage. Blossoms are very large.

XXX.   (Opposite) Garden Party is rich ivory at the heart, blending int
apple-blossom pink. A good hybrid tea to use with shell to deep pinks an
soft yellows.

XXXI.   *Tiffany has deep-pink, long-pointed buds with beautiful form and long strong stems.*

XXXII. (Above) Gail Borden is a lovely bi-color hybrid tea that produces large blossoms excellent for exhibition.

XXXIII. (Left) The Farmer's Wife has deep-pink flowers which open slowly and are long-lasting when cut for arrangements.

XXXIV-XXXVI. *(Opposite) Good floribundas in the pale to deep orange range are Ginger (above, left) whose flowers are long lasting; Woburn Abbey (below) with blossoms that combine orange tones of red, and a golden yellow reverse, and Peach Glow (below) with golden coral blooms suffused with pink at the base. Although color is a matter of taste, of course, these would be pleasant harmony in any garden or flower arrangement.*

XXXVII. *Tanya has red-orange buds which become a radiant orange when fully open. This high-centered rose with a classic tea form was used in the arrangement (Plate 70) which won the 1959 Sterling Bowl Tournament.*

9

A ROSE IS FOREVER

*Drye roses put to the nose to smell
do comforte the braine and the harte
and quencheth the Spirits.*

ROGER ASCHAM
1515-1568 A.D.

*It (the rose) has made its way, as we have
said, into ointments. By itself it possesses
medicinal properties. It is an ingredient of
plasters and of eye-salves by reason of its
subtle pungency, even being used as a
coating for the delicacies of our tables, being
quite harmless.*

PLINY, THE ELDER
23-79 A.D.

F or many rose fanciers a rose is more than an ornamental flower. A rose is to eat ... to drink ... to smell long after the blooms have vanished from the garden ... and to those who preserve their blooms in silica gel, a rose is forever.

The English diarist, Samuel Pepys, confided a gleeful tidbit about an acquaintance who quaffed a glass of rose wine and promptly jumped out of a second-story window. Concluded Pepys, "The desperatist frolic I did ever see."

In the Persian book, *Gulistan* (the title means "Rose Garden"), the recipe is given for a rose wine which is guaranteed to be so potent that "a glass could make the sternest monarch merciful or make the sickliest mortal slumber amid his pains." Even in those days, it seems, men had to find good and sufficient reasons to justify their drinking habits.

Among the early Romans, a glass of wine could only be appreciated to its fullest when afloat with a fragrant, full-blown rose. The Romans of today make a brew called *Sangue di Rosa* (Rose's Blood) that is claimed to be not only inebriating but also to have an aphrodisiac effect. Another common belief in the early Roman day was that a crown of roses, worn from the first sip to final intoxication, would reduce a monumental hangover to a day-after state of euphoria. According to Athenaeus, a crown of roses not only possessed the property of alleviating pain in the head but also had a definite refreshing effect. And in this he had the support of two prominent Greek physicians, Mnesitheus and Callimachus.

ROSE AS A PANACEA

As the years passed, more and more benefits were discovered. In the sixteenth century the Swiss philosopher and physician, Paracelsus, said, "Flowers that are of a burning color like the rose are apt to heal inflammations; those which bear the color of a face heated by wine, as the rose does, obviate drunkenness."

In the middle of the next century Nicholas Culpeper in his *Complete Herbal* went further. "The white and red roses are cooling and drying, and yet the white is taken to exceed the red in both the properties, but is seldom used inwardly in any medicine...

"Red roses do strengthen the heart, the stomach and the liver and the retentive faculty: they mitigate the pains that arise from heat, assuage inflammations, procure rest and sleep: the juice of them doth purge and cleanse the body from choler and phlegm. The husks of the roses, with the beards and nails of the roses, are binding and cooling and the distilled water of either of them is good for the heart and redness in the eyes, and to stay and dry up the rheums and watering of them."

In his *Paradisus,* written in 1629, John Parkinson stated: "The Rose is of exceeding great use with us; for the Damaske Rose (besides the super-excellent sweete water it yeeldeth being distilled, or the perfume of the leaves being dryed, serving to fill sweet bags) serveth to cause solubleness of the body, made into a Syrupe, or preserved with Sugar moist or dry candied.... The White Rose is much used for the cooling of heate in the eyes; divers doe make an excellent yellow color of the juyce of white Roses, wherein some Allome is dissolved, to colour flowers or pictures."

Another seventeenth century writer recommended red roses for invigorating "the liver, kidneys, and other weak intrails," and as a specific to "strengthen the heart and helpe the trembling thereof."

If all the curative powers attributed to the rose actually existed it would have reduced our present-day wonder drugs to the level of aspirin. Little did the early physicians realize that while the physical properties of the rose were limited, its curative powers from a psychological aspect were of far greater significance. Hippocrates prescribed rose perfumes for the nervous disorders of his patients and the Greek poet Anacreon wrote:

> "The rose distills a healing balm
> The beating pulse of pain to calm."

ROSE HIPS   Despite the extravagant claims there is some basis for citing curative powers of a limited sort. During World War II the British found that rose hips

78.   *(Opposite) Until a century ago, apothecaries placed great store on the therapeutic values of rose leaves, rose petals and rose hips which were used in a wide variety of formulations.*

contain 400 times as much vitamin C as oranges. As a result vast quantities were collected by Boy Scouts and converted into a syrup.

Rose hips are the fruit of the plant. They occur after a flower has been fertilized and seeds develop. These are contained in a pod that is called the *rose hip*.

In his book, *The Rose, Its History, Poetry, Culture and Classification*, the American writer, S. B. Parsons, reported in 1865 a chemical analysis of the petals of the Provence rose which revealed: "Vegetable matter and essential oil, gallic acid, coloring matter, albumen, tannin, some salts with a base of potash or chalk, silex and oxyde of iron." Since this rose is quite bitter, he concluded, "A small dose (of the dried petals) in powders strengthens the stomach and assists digestion," while "a conserve of any variety is excellent in cases of colds or catarrh." Few doctors would agree with the latter statement.

FIRST COLD CREAM

The more common and also more beneficial qualities of the rose that have come down to us involve its use as a food and in the preparation of perfumes. Actually the first cold cream was discovered by the Greek physician Galen who lived a century before Christ. He suggested, "Melt four ounces of white wax in a pound of rose oil. Stir in a little cold water very gradually to give it a clear and opaque whiteness. Wash this mixture in rose water, and add small quantities of rose water and rose vinegar to make it the right consistency."

ROSE PERFUME

The essence or attar of roses is used extensively in the perfume industry today. The two main centers for its production are at Grasse in France and in The Valley of Roses in Bulgaria.

Just when the distillation process, by which the attar is extracted, was discovered is hard to say. Some claim that it was known to the Greeks and Romans but the fact that Pliny has little to say on this subject would indicate that their knowledge was limited to the production of the rose water, which they used so extensively.

The distillation process was discovered by accident according to another version. Father Catron in his *History of the Mogul Empire*, wrote that the Sultana Nur Mahal was entertaining the great Mogul Jehan-guire. She had a canal on which they were sailing filled with rose water. During the heat of mid-afternoon they noticed a froth floating on the surface of the water. They collected some of it and found it to be intensely fragrant. The heat of the sun had caused the attar to separate from the water and form a scum.

The Princess was not only beautiful but ambitious. Soon after she had made her impression on the Mogul, five of his favorite wives died mysteriously and she became the Empress. Subsequently Nur Mahal arranged for her niece, Mumtaz Mahal, to marry the heir to the throne. It was for Mumtaz that the Taj Mahal, the most beautiful tomb in the world, was built.

ROSES IN COOKING

Roses are frequently used in cooking but a recipe credited by Athenaeus to the cook of the King of Sicily provides a delicacy that requires a highly educated palate. "This is what I call potted roses, and it is thus prepared: I first pound some of the most fragrant roses in a mortar; then I take the brains of birds and pigs, well boiled and stripped of every particle of meat; I then add the yolks of some eggs, some oil, a little cordial, some pepper, and some wine: after having beaten and mixed it well together, I throw it in a new pot, and place it over a slow but steady fire." As he said this, the story goes, "the cook uncovered the pot, and there issued forth a most delicious fragrance, perfuming the whole dining hall and overcoming the guests with delight."

Some more acceptable recipes, both old and new, include the following:

HAGEBUTTEN SUPPE (ROSE-HIP SOUP)

½ pound dried rose hips   2 ounces potato flour (or potato starch)
3 pints cold water   Sugar to taste

Wash the hips, soak them some hours in water, let them simmer until quite soft, then pass through a sieve. Boil up again, adding sugar, thicken with potato flour and serve, either with or without noodles or little dumplings. Time of preparation, one hour. Serves six persons.

LOZENGES OF RED ROSES

Boyl your sugar to sugar again then put in your red roses, being finely beaten and mayd moist with the juice of a lemon. Let it not boyl after the Roses are in, but pour it upon a Pye plate and cut it into what form you please.

SWEETBRIAR ROSE HIP JAM

2 cups hips, before seeding   1 cup water
1½ cups sugar   2 tablespoons lemon juice

Prepare hips and measure 1 cup. Boil sugar and water 4 minutes, add hips and lemon juice, cover and boil 15 minutes; uncover and boil 5 minutes more. The berries should be clear and transparent and the syrup thick. When done, pour into hot sterilized glasses and seal. If hips are very ripe before frost has touched them, add more lemon juice to each cup of hips.

HONEY OF ROSES

Cut the white heels from red roses. (The heel looks like a white cuticle at the base of the petal. It is bitter and should be removed.) Take half a pound of them and put them into a stone jar, and pour on them 3 pints of boiling water. Stir well and let them stand 12 hours. Then press off the liquor and when it has settled add to it 5 pounds of honey. Boil it well, and when it is of the consistency of a thick syrup it is ready to put away.

HAREM KISSES

½ cup red rose petals

1 egg white

1½ tablespoons water

3 tablespoons light cream

Confectioners' sugar

Remove the bitter base from the petals and blend with egg white, water and light cream until smooth and fluffy. Pour into a mixing bowl and gradually add sifted confectioners' sugar until the mixture is thick enough to knead. Work it until smooth then cover with a damp cloth. Allow to stand for an hour and shape into small balls. Top each ball with an almond.

CANDIED ROSE PETALS

Slightly beat one egg white in a small bowl. Sprinkle a layer of sugar on a small plate. Dip rose petals and leaves first in egg-white and then in sugar so they are coated on both sides. Dry on rack. Store dried petals and leaves on waxpaper, each layer separated by paper toweling. Use on candy tray, as garnish for fruit cup, as decoration on cakes or as border for cake plate. Decorative and delicious too.

Bon Appetit!

DRIED ROSES

The silica gel process of drying flowers was originated by Dorothea Thompson, author of *Creative Decorations with Dried Flowers,* published by Hearthside Press. Silica gel is a chemical that looks and feels like ordinary table salt. It is packaged especially for drying flowers under the trade name of Flower-Dri and sold at many garden supply centers and florist shops. Silica gel never wears out; you can use it over and over again.

Mrs. Thompson's directions for drying roses follow:

Select a wide-mouthed container—a large jar or candy tin is fine. Sprinkle a layer of silica gel one-half inch deep in the jar. Lay rose buds horizontally on the bottom. Pour in silica gel to cover them completely. Add another layer of buds or open flowers (use flowers only three-quarters open). Cover with silica gel. Repeat until you have filled the container, ending with a top layer of silica gel.

After about a week gently brush off the chemical and remove the roses. They should be completely dry by then.

Mrs. Thompson recommends that if using open roses (remember, no more than three-quarters open) you cut the sepals close to the receptacle before drying (they curl when dry). After the flower is dry attach a wire stem as for a corsage.

79. *Roses and foliage to be dried are shown on a bed of silica gel. The blossoms are laid at a 45° angle.*

To strengthen a dried rose (or to patch a rose if petals should fall) apply a few drops of Elmer's or Sobo glue to the bottom where the petals are attached to the receptacle. Spread the glue thinly with a toothpick. Allow to dry before you remove any silica gel which may have adhered to the dried rose.

To make dried roses less brittle, spray with clear plastic spray or dip in warm melted paraffin.

After following this drying procedure once, it is simple to repeat. The results are almost unbelievable.

POTPOURRI

The derivation of the word *potpourri* (pronounced po-poo-re), is strangely at variance with the real thing. Most of us think of potpourri as a fragrant mixture of rose petals and assorted herbs, which it is. But the term is made up of the French words, *pot,* meaning a container, and the verb *pourrir,* to rot. The crock or jar used in making potpourri is thus a rotting jar—which must come as a jolt to anyone who enjoys the final results. The process used to preserve the essential oils that provide rose fragrance is based on the rotting or fermentation of rose petals, hence the phrase.

Four interesting medieval recipes are mentioned by Bonnie Roberson in the 1962 *American Rose Annual.* She points out that color of the blooms is of no importance but that the flowers should be picked when newly opened, before they have lost their scent.

CURING THE PETALS

A heaping tablespoon of salt should be sprinkled on each quart of petals and thoroughly mixed in with a wooden spoon. A plate or non-metallic weight should be placed on top to press the petals down in the rotting jar. If any mold appears add a little more salt and mix in well. Also, if liquid forms remove the weight until it is all evaporated. After a month a fixative should be added, such as cut and dried orris root (a cup to 2 quarts of petals). When all visible liquid is gone, break the petals into small pieces and use as the base for any of the following four blends.

BLEND NO. 1

1 quart cured petals	½ teaspoon crushed mace
½ teaspoon crushed nutmeg	½ teaspoon crushed allspice
½ teaspoon crushed cinnamon	1 cup dried thyme
½ teaspoon crushed cloves	¼ cup powdered benzoin (fixative)

1   dram rose oil, if desired (may be obtained at a drug or specialty food store)

80. *The ingredients for exotic potions would be carefully weighed on apothecary scales according to minute directions printed by long-forgotten physicians.*

BLEND NO. 2

1 quart cured petals	1 cup dried clary-sage (fixative)
1 teaspoon nutmeg	1 cup dried marjoram
1 teaspoon cinnamon	½ cup calamus root (fixative)
2 cups lavender flowers	1 dram oil sweet-orange

BLEND NO. 3

1 quart cured petals	1 cup vetiver root, cut (fixative)
1 teaspoon cloves, crushed	1 cup lemon verbena leaves
1 teaspoon cardamom, crushed	1 vanilla bean, cut
1 cup dried lemon balm	1 dram oil of jasmine

BLEND NO. 4

1 cup cured petals	1 cup gum benzoin
1 tablespoon nutmeg	1 cup dried rosemary
1 cup vetiver root	½ cup dried orange peel
1 cup sandalwood shavings	1 dram oil of thyme

To mix, measure 1 quart of cured rose petals, well broken, into an enameled pan. Add all other ingredients and mix well with hands. Place in a glass jar with tight-fitting lid and shake well once or twice daily to help blend.

After a 4- to 6-month fermentation period the potpourri should be ready for use. A tablespoon of brandy or any other unscented alcohol will increase the evaporation rate making the fragrance more readily available.

DRY METHOD   The dry method for preparing potpourri is just as simple as the moist. Remove petals from newly opened rose blossoms and spread on cheese cloth or newspaper. Leave for two weeks in a warm, dry area away from the sun. Then mix with other ingredients mentioned in the four blends and store in the dark in airtight containers for about two months. The mixture will then be ready for use and may be transferred to more decorative jars.

FIXATIVES   These substances are used to capture the volatile oils of the rose and prevent them from evaporating. It is best to use vegetable fixatives, such as orris root, gum benzoin or vetiver rather than the animal fixatives—civet, ambergris or musk. The vegetable types are less expensive and easier to obtain. If they come in the root form they must be ground. Most are available in powder form from the prescription department of any good drug store. Vetiver may come as an oil and should be used sparingly since it is highly concentrated in this form.

10

A ROSE IS A PICTURE

Oh, there is naught in nature bright,
Where Roses do not shed their light!
Where morning paints the orient skies,
Her fingers burn with roseate dyes!
ANACREON
563-478 B.C.

A rose is one of the easiest subjects to photograph, if you merely want a pleasing picture, but one of the hardest if you need a faithful color reproduction. It is easy because it is saturated with color, and hard because some of the colors are difficult to capture accurately.

If you were to set yourself the task of producing an encyclopedia of rose pictures which would be recognized throughout the world as true to color, you would fail. In fact, you could not succeed even if you limited yourself to the United States. The color of a rose varies with the time of day, with the season, with climate and even with the soil in which the plant is grown. Naturally, incandescent light will produce a color different from daylight and must be compensated for by using appropriate film. But the amount or quality of daylight will also have a bearing on color accuracy, as will the color temperature of artificial light.

Some of the problems are best illustrated by examples.

LAVENDER ROSES

A number of years ago the Jackson & Perkins Company introduced a lavender rose called Sterling Silver. For one picture it was decided to have two handsome bouquets of the Sterling Silver rose placed on either side of a wedding cake decorated with sugar roses dyed the same shade of lavender. The match between the sugar roses and the actual blooms was nearly perfect, so the picture was taken using Eastman Ektachrome film. On the resulting transparency the sugar roses were a beautiful lavender but the real flowers were a magenta pink! Eventually it was found that best results were achieved outdoors by photographing Sterling

81. *The seemingly simple picture on the right was the result of a full day's work by one of the photographic teams which Peter Braal, Manager of the Photographic Illustration Division of Eastman Kodak, sends world-wide to create illustrations for the giant Colorama in Grand Central Station in New York City. The cameraman is Don Marvin. Assisting him are Walter Latoski, art director, and Dick King, photo assistant, holding the reflector. The man with his back to the camera is the author.*

XXXVIII. *Photographed with the floribunda Junior Miss is the young lady, Linda Felber, who won the national title of Junior Miss in 1964. (Photographed on Ektacolor/ASA 80/; one second at f.45 using 8 × 10 Deardorf camera. Foil reflector was used to light shadow detail and catch light in model's eyes.)*

XXXIX.   *The hybrid tea John F. Kennedy was named as a living memorial to our late President. To reduce the yellow tinge that is normal in photographs of white roses, two color compensating filters (CC10B plus CC05B) were used. (Film: Daylight Ektachrome/ASA 50/; 1/60 of a second at f.20 using a 4 × 5 Deardorf camera. Strobe lighting, Ascor 600, comprised two front lights and one rear. Photographer, Richard Marshall.)*

XL.   *(Opposite) The technique of using blooms in sharp focus in the foreground, with the background in soft focus, is typical of the work of Vincent Lisanti who, in this case, wished to emphasize Kordes Perfecta, the first variety to be named the Rose of the Year (1959).*

XLI-XLVIII. *At the Hallmark Gallery exhibit in New York the rose was depicted in literature, art, music, design, ornament, legend, medicine, and food. Popular with photography fans was a series of niches that had un-*

usual backgrounds designed to bring out the qualities of different varieties
of roses. In each case a single blossom was displayed in a bud vase with
hidden lighting that gave a dramatic effect to both bloom and background.

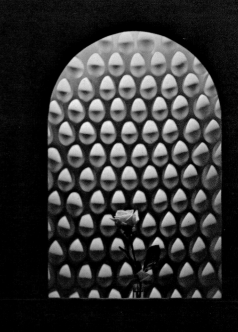

XLIX, L.   A part of the 17-acre Jackson & Perkins display rose garden at Newark, New York, where more than 36,000 rose plants bloom continuously from June until Fall frosts. Constant bloom is achieved by removing one third of the stems from each plant in Spring. This forces new bottom breaks which produce another crop of flowers after the initial burst of bloom has ended. The two roses in the foreground are hybrid tea Bermudiana (also shown in detail on opposite page) and behind it, Golden Masterpiece.

LI.   (Above) Blossoms in the lower left frame the composition and lead the eye directly into the center of interest.

LII.   (Below) The camera was placed slightly higher than the level of the rose blooms. As a result the flowers appear close together and provide maximum color.

Silver at noon on a heavily overcast day (when the light is coldest).

The problem was so intriguing that Eastman's Professional Technical Center, under the direction of Philip Sidney, decided to experiment. The rose was photographed in a studio using controlled lighting and color negative. A series of graduated prints were made on Ektacolor paper. When these were studied it was found that one gradation was true to color when compared with the rose in daylight, and that an entirely different gradation illustrated the rose under artificial lighting. Imagine the additional problems in the printing of rose illustrations where the color transparency must be transferred to ink and paper! One control commonly used is a viewing box which permits varying mixtures of daylight and artificial light for illuminating transparencies. Once the correct color is achieved readings are taken on each dial and sent to the printer, who has a similar machine. By duplicating the readings he can learn the exact color he is expected to reproduce on paper.

WHITE ROSES

White is another difficult rose color. To the eye the John F. Kennedy hybrid tea rose appears pure white when fully open. But unless a filter is used it always photographs with a definite yellow tinge, even with the use of strobe lighting which is cool and goes deep into the rose, softening the shadows. Inside the bloom are yellow stamens which the eye cannot see but the film evidently does.

Sometimes the apparent color variation is due to an untrained eye. For instance, an artist painting a snow scene knows that shadows are not black but blue. Perhaps there is some correlation between this fact and a color oddity discovered in the Eastman studio. Whenever a particular blue background was required a piece of black velvet was used. For some unknown reason it always came out on the film as a rich royal blue!

CORAL ROSES

There is no explanation as to why the coral-orange floribunda, Fashion, rarely photographs as the eye sees it. However, anyone unfamiliar with the true color would doubtless be happy with a pleasing picture that might impress fellow photographers, although disappointing rose growers.

MASS PLANTINGS

Disregarding composition for the moment, the angle or camera-point-of-view is all important when taking a color photograph of an extensive rose planting. For instance, there are more than 36,000 rose bushes in the Jackson & Perkins display garden at Newark, New York, but aerial color pictures of this garden have always been disappointing, to say the least. The reason is that the camera is looking

82. (*Opposite, above*) *If many of the flowers on the plant are spent, move the camera in close and focus on a small cluster of perfect blooms.*

83. (*Opposite, below*) *Bright color in the foreground helps to provide the illusion of colorful blooms throughout the entire vista.*

84. (*Above*) *It is customary to eliminate shadows in rose arrangement pictures, but there are times when shadows can be effective. Here they aid in giving balance.*

almost straight down and no matter how many blooms there are, they are bound to be separated by a lot of green leaves and brown earth. The trick is to line up the camera so that it is slightly higher than the general level of the blooms. This pulls them together and provides maximum color saturation. Even so, it is wise to select a bed of bright-colored roses with lots of blooms for the foreground. Even if close inspection shows that there is a sparsity of color in the background of the photograph the brightness of the foreground will give the illusion of bounteous color throughout the garden.

FRAME THE PICTURE

The technique of using sharply defined, bright color in the foreground is even more effective if the picture is framed by a rose arbor, by a pillar rose on one side, or either a floribunda hedge with masses of color or a climber trained on a fence across the lower portion of the picture. If none of these is available it is still possible to arrange a few perfect blooms so that they will fill a lower corner of the frame and provide a signature, as it were, for the overall picture. Assuming that you are working from a ground glass with the camera on a tripod the blooms may be positioned on another tripod just below the range of vision. This permits moving them around until the composition is precisely as you want it. Incidentally, a tripod and ground glass are highly recommended; if close-up pictures are to be taken, they are almost mandatory. It is possible to get pictures of single roses by using a wire focal frame attached to the camera or even a piece of string stretched from the lens to measure the proper focal distance. But so many things can happen to ruin a beautiful picture—camera motion or poor composition— so it pays to work with a tripod and see on the ground glass exactly what you are getting.

MOVE IN CLOSE

In every bed of roses there are some blooms that are past their peak and unless you have permission to clean them out their flowers are likely to detract from an otherwise beautiful picture. The easiest way to avoid this is to move in close and select a single bloom, a nice arrangement of three or four flowers, or possibly a floribunda candelabra-type cluster. Here you may choose to use a wide aperture so that the desired blooms are sharply focused but other flowers and leaves go out of focus making soft splotches of background color. The effect is pleasing and almost surrealistic.

ISOLATE THE FLOWER

Another method is to isolate the flowers by placing cardboard of either neutral gray or a complementary color in the background. If the cardboard is blue and is meant to simulate sky, then make sure that no shadows fall on it. A simpler way, if you can cut the flowers, is to anchor them in a needlepoint holder raised so that the best part of the sky forms the background. If you want clouds for the background, pick the right day and using your needlepoint holder compose the picture where the clouds are best. Make your shot quickly before they change. With proper placement the blooms may be made to appear as though coming off a high climber.

DEW DROPS

Some photographers cannot take a close-up picture of a rose unless it is thoroughly doused with water. This fake dew is supposed to enhance the rose. I say it is corny and the devil with it. But if you are intrigued with the idea, then get up early and catch the roses with real dew on them and with the light cutting across at a low slant. If this is asking too much then fill a small plastic nasal-spray container with water and squirt away. Get it out of your system and go on to better things.

ROSE PORTRAITS

If you are willing to take the time and make the effort there are a number of ways to take rose portraits that will be different from those of your neighbor.

For instance, use a bare picture frame to enclose the best part of a rose bush. This works very well with tree roses because here you have a nice clustered effect at eye level and you don't have to stoop or muddy your knees. Arrange at least one stem so that it crosses over the edge of the frame.

MONTAGE

A photo montage can be made using either one variety of rose or two or more colors in combination. Stretch chicken wire across the top of a shallow baking pan containing enough water to keep the roses in good condition while the picture is being arranged and photographed. Drop the stems through holes in the wire grid and move the blooms around until you have a composition that both pleases you and hides any sign of the mechanics. This type of picture is most effective when the roses "bleed" off all edges, or in other words, when the entire picture is filled with roses.

Another variation might be to select an attractive shallow bowl and float rose blooms on it. Here you can allow the dish and even the bottom, if it is attractive, to show through. Water, when not in sweaty beads, generally adds to a rose picture so you might try floating blossoms in a small garden pool. In each case you should position the camera either directly overhead or at a fairly steep angle looking down on the composition.

85. *A simple black background provides a dramatic setting for a portrait of a single pale rose.*

ACCESSORIES THAT CONNOTE MEANING

A simple accessory that connotes the name or an outstanding characteristic of the rose can help make a rose portrait more effective. The John F. Kennedy rose picture in catalogs features a bronze bust of the late President. A gold cup was used with the All-America floribunda, Gold Cup, and the Manhattan skyline with the red hybrid tea, New Yorker. It is hard to fail if you use animals or pretty girls. The 1967 All-America floribunda, Gay Princess, was used to make a crown for the former Newark Rose Festival Princess, 8-year-old Brenda Claflin. An attractive Tahitian girl wearing roses in her hair posed for a picture with the 1962 Rose of the Year, South Seas, while a glass horse was photographed beside an arrangement of the 1964 All-America floribunda, Saratoga, to associate it with the famous Saratoga Racetrack.

SPECIAL EQUIPMENT

With special equipment you can make unusual pictures of roses by presenting them in an unfamiliar setting. For instance, Frank Bauman, photographer for *Look* magazine used an extension tube so that his pictures went right into the heart of the current Rose of the Year, Mexicana, to show the center with its brilliant color bleeding off on all sides. Vic Keppler, Director of the Famous Photographers' School, designed two tubes, one glass and the other aluminum, and had both made to fit over his lens. Pictures taken through these tubes show the blossom sharp in the center of the picture while the colors, reflected from the sides of the tubes, swirl around until they finally go completely out of the frame. The famous horticultural photographers, Sam Gottscho and his son-in-law, the late Bill Schleisner, photographed several varieties of roses behind different types of glass. Their pictures resembled paintings more than photographs.

Simplicity is the keynote of all good photographs. It is especially important with roses where the flower itself should predominate—anything else should serve only as a background, or accessory. There are several ways to provide effective but unobtrusive backgrounds: pieces of velvet tacked to a board, a roll of bamboo window blind, sheets of colored cardboard or rolls of colored paper, ordinary window shades—white, gray and black—and a large bed sheet. Several special effects can be achieved by stretching a sheet tight and throwing light on it from behind. A blue light may simulate blue sky, for instance. Similarly, Venetian blinds which allow light to filter through can provide backlighting as well as strong horizontal lines that will enhance a rose portrait.

HELPFUL MECHANICS

Among your accessories include some of those used by flower arrangers. Needlepoint holders are invaluable for holding rose stems in position. The lead bases

86. *A still-life study of the Hallmark hybrid tea rose features a Mexican chest.*

will permit you to anchor the stem with the rose at just the right angle while the flower is kept fresh by standing in water. A glaring "hole" in a rose bush or bed can be filled with color by adding cut flowers from another plant of the same variety. Keep them fresh by putting them in water-filled glass tubes taped to green florist stakes. The stick will make it easier to put each bloom in the proper place, but both stick and tube should be hidden from view. The flower arranger's twistems make it simple to attach the tube or to pull closer together rose stems that are too far apart. A thin wire can also be slipped inside the length of a rose stem to bend the flower into the precise position needed for your composition—and you need not worry about its staying in place.

HOW TO POSE THE FLOWER

Posing the flower is especially important with roses. The most attractive stage is when the bloom is three-quarters open and the best angle is one looking partly into the high center. This means either elevating the camera or leaning the flower toward the lens. This is where the thin wire may come in handy.

If you wish to escape the vagaries of wind, move indoors to make your color pictures. Be sure to cut the blooms during the preceding afternoon. Put them in cold water and store in a cool place in the cellar or better still, in a refrigerator where the temperature is about 34 degrees F. This will harden them off so that they will last longer under the hot lights.

Also anticipate and make allowances for the following problem. Your light meter reading naturally will be taken from the blooms. If they are very pale the foliage will not receive enough exposure. A baby spotlight directed on the leaves will help correct this deficiency. An overhead light will provide the basic lighting and other lights may be used as needed to avoid flat lighting or too heavy shadows.

FLOWER ARRANGEMENT PICTURES

The main problems that arise when photographing flower arrangements are reflection from containers, accessories or the backboard. Shadows can also distort a composition. The ideal lighting arrangement is a series of flood lights that permit balancing the light, that is, adjusting to eliminate shadows and flare back while illuminating the arrangement as a whole. For instance, one light for the background, one off to one side and the third for the opposite side. When this is not possible and a flash attachment is the only source of light, the best procedure is to use bounce light. By pointing the flash up to the ceiling the only light used on the arrangement is that which is reflected from above. This type of illumination is not as strong as direct flash but is less likely to cause strong shadows and distorting glare.

If you wish to see your photographs published then study and practice the following points.

1. Most publishers prefer 4 × 5 color transparencies rather than 35 mm.

2. Black and white pictures should have plenty of contrast in a good range of tones from white through various grays to black.

3. Calendars generally demand vertical pictures; books, magazines and newspapers can use both vertical and horizontal.

4. Avoid cutting into the base, container, plant material or anything that is an element of the overall design. In fact, allow at least one inch on all sides of the composition so that the editor may be free to crop the picture as needed.

5. The best color for the background is a pale neutral gray. But if the arrangement already has a dark background then there is not much you can do about it.

6. Remove all labels, ribbons and awards from the composition.

7. Inspect the composition minutely. There are many reasons why pictures are rejected: a crease in a tablecloth; flowers that are no longer fresh; a niche hinge that appears awkward. Don't expose your film until fully satisfied that the composition is perfect in every detail.

8. When you have a good black and white print don't mar it by writing on the back.

BLACK AND WHITE PICTURES

If you are photographing in black and white, your main problem will be separating the tones. With monochrome film, reds and greens often reproduce as the same shade of gray. A red lens filter will lighten a dark red rose and separate it from the leaves. (Without the filter the blossoms are likely to disappear into the green foliage.) Since this is not a color photograph few people will be aware that the dark red rose appears lighter than normal. Unless you are familiar with the fundamentals of films and filters you would be wise to obtain a book specializing in this subject. Then select one kind of film and stay with it until you are thoroughly familiar with its assets and limitations.

HOW TO IMPROVE YOUR COMPOSITION

The quality of many amateur pictures indicates that some photographers have difficulty in achieving good composition. A rule of thumb, discovered almost five centuries before Christ by the Greek Pythagoras, can be helpful. Like any other rule, it is made to be broken on occasion but for the most part it works quite well. The story goes that there was a contest in Greece to decide the ideal point at which to divide a line of any given length into the two most beautifully proportioned parts. Pythagoras, who was both a philosopher and a mathematician, won the contest by stating that any separation in the area lying between one-quarter and one-third of the length would result in the greatest harmony between the two parts.

87.   *The floribunda Saratoga with two glass models of horses.*

88, 89. *The technique of using background to illustrate or connote the names of roses is shown in these pictures. (Left) These roses are anchored in needlepoint holders to position them for photography. (Right) New Yorker with the city background.*

Therefore if you have a horizontal line, whether sky at the top, grass or a fairly solid color line at the bottom, position the dominant line in the Pythagorean area. In the same measure, if you have strong vertical lines—a pillar rose, tree, part of a house, a wall or a solid green area, a figurine or piece of sculpture—again try to place the strongest line in this area. At all costs avoid having the focal point of interest at the exact center of the picture. Move it off center and try to compose other elements to lead the eye directly to the focal point. For instance, a path beginning at one corner might lead toward the focal point. It need not to be anything so obvious as a path but experience and tender loving attention to your ground glass will help you learn the elements that will make your pictures simple, direct, forceful and filled with the basic beauty of good proportion.

11
ROSE AWARDS

In the form and color, sweetness, grace—
None with the Rose could once compare:
She bore the palm in Flora's eyes,
Who to the Rose adjudged the prize.
                    S. B. PARSONS
                    1847

R̲ose awards are an indication of the value of a particular variety but it is important to remember that some very good roses are not on any award list. This is usually due to the high cost of development and the need to put a rose on the market quickly rather than wait out the trial period needed for a particular award.

While criteria for judging roses tend to vary, any system that requires testing in all climatic areas of America is bound to eliminate the variety that performs well only in a restricted area.

The outstanding American award systems are outlined in the following pages together with all the roses honored by each system.

AMERICAN ROSE SOCIETY RATINGS

Space precludes the listing here of the roses rated by members of the American Rose Society in their annual Proof of the Pudding. (Obtaining this yearly list is another very good reason for joining the Society.) Individual members give varieties scores which then are averaged out on a national basis. The highest potential score is 10 though no rose has ever attained this peak. This system is more valuable for the well-established older roses since it takes time for members to obtain and try out the new varieties and even more time before there are sufficient reports on a specific rose for the ratings to become meaningful.

On occasion the Society also chooses outstanding roses for the American Rose Society Gold Certificates. However, the Certificate is not awarded on a regular schedule as is indicated by the dates of the awards made so far.

GOLD CERTIFICATE AWARDS

		CLASS	INTRODUCER
1961	Spartan Orange-red	Floribunda	Jackson & Perkins
	Montezuma Salmon-red	Grandiflora	Armstrong
1960	Queen Elizabeth Clear pink	Grandiflora	Germain's
1958	Golden Wings Sulphur-yellow	Hybrid Tea	Bosley
1956	Vogue Cherry-coral	Floribunda	Jackson & Perkins
	Chrysler Imperial Crimson-red	Hybrid Tea	Germain's
1955	Frensham Deep scarlet	Floribunda	Conard-Pyle
1954	Fashion Coral-pink	Floribunda	Jackson & Perkins
	Carrousel Pink-red	Grandiflora	Elmer Roses
1950	City of New York Creamy white	Rambler	Conard-Pyle
1948	Peace Creamy yellow with flush pink	Hybrid Tea	Conard-Pyle

THE ROSE OF THE YEAR

Among the color pictures in this book are illustrations of the eight roses that have been chosen for the annual Rose of the Year award. These are selected by a panel of 15,000 home rose gardeners located in most of the states.

YEAR	VARIETY	HYBRIDIST	COUNTRY
1966	Mexicana Bi-color, red with silver reverse	E. S. Boerner	U.S.A.
1965	Polynesian Sunset Coral-orange	E. S. Boerner	U.S.A.
1964	World's Fair Salute Crimson-red	Dennison Morey	U.S.A.
1963	Tropicana Orange-red	Mathias Tantau	Germany

YEAR	VARIETY	HYBRIDIST	COUNTRY
1962	South Seas Coral-pink	Dennison Morey	U.S.A.
1961	Americana Bright red	E. S. Boerner	U.S.A.
1960	Hawaii Orange-coral blend	E. S. Boerner	U.S.A.
1959	Kordes Perfecta Bi-color, creamy white with carmine on petal edges	Wilhelm Kordes	Germany

INTERNATIONAL ROSE TEST GARDENS

The International Rose Test Gardens at Portland, Oregon, began judging roses in 1919. The Curator, R. E. Kalmbach, and a panel of judges score new roses each year and select those varieties that perform best in the Portland garden. Gold medal winners over the years include:

YEAR	VARIETY	ORIGINATOR	COUNTRY
1965	Orangeade Orange	McGredy	Ireland
1964	Matterhorn White	Armstrong	U.S.A.
1964	Silver Lining Silvery	Dickson	N. Ireland
1964	Wendy Cussons Rose-red	Gregory	England
1963	Mischief Salmon	McGredy	Ireland
1962	Chicago Peace Bi-color, pink, yellow	Conard-Pyle	U.S.A.
1961	Tropicana Orange-red	Tantau	Germany
1961	Royal Highness Clear pink	Conard-Pyle	U.S.A.
1960	Golden Slippers Orange-gold	Peterson & Dering	U.S.A.
1960	Memoriam Pastel pink	Peterson & Dering	U.S.A.
1959	El Capitan Cherry-red	Howard Rose Co.	U.S.A.

YEAR	VARIETY	ORIGINATOR	COUNTRY
1959	Angel Wings Bi-color, yellow, pink	Howard Rose Co.	U.S.A.
1959	Pink Parfait Light pink	Armstrong	U.S.A.
1957	Little Darling Red-orange	McGredy	Ireland
1957	Kordes Perfecta Bi-color, creamy white, carmine	Kordes	Germany
1957	Sarabande Scarlet-orange	Meilland	France
1956	Burnaby Yellow	Eddie	Canada
1956	Audie Murphy Cherry-red	Lammerts	U.S.A.
1956	Pink Favorite Pink	Von Abrams	U.S.A.
1956	Montezuma Salmon-red	Swim	U.S.A.
1956	Golden Showers Yellow	Lammerts	U.S.A.
1955	Mrs. Sam McGredy Scarlet-orange	McGredy	Ireland
1955	McGredy's Yellow Yellow	McGredy	Ireland
1954	Spartan Orange-red	Boerner	U.S.A.
1954	Carrousel Pink-red	Duehrsen	U.S.A.
1954	Ena Harkness Crimson-scarlet	Norman	England
1953	Tiffany Orchid-pink	Lindquist	U.S.A.
1953	Queen Elizabeth Clear pink	Lammerts	U.S.A.
1952	Independence Scarlet	Kordes	Germany
1951	Chrysler Imperial Crimson-red	Lammerts	U.S.A.
1950	Vogue Cherry-coral	Boerner	U.S.A.

YEAR	VARIETY	ORIGINATOR	COUNTRY
1949	Fashion Coral-pink	Boerner	U.S.A.
1947	Forty-Niner Bi-color—red, yellow	Swim	U.S.A.
1946	Sutter's Gold Golden yellow	Swim	U.S.A.
1945	Rubaiyat Cerise-red	McGredy	Ireland
⟵ 1944	Peace Creamy yellow with flush pink	Meilland	France
1944	Lowell Thomas Butter yellow	Mallerin	France
1941	Neville Chamberlain Salmon	Lens	Belgium
1941	Grand Duchesse Charlotte Wine red	Ketten	Luxembourg
1941	Dickson's Red Scarlet-red	Dickson	Ireland
1941	Dainty Maid Silvery pink	Le Grice	England
1941	Heart's Desire Deep rose-red	Howard & Smith	U.S.A.
1941	Charlotte Armstrong Cerise-red	Lammerts	U.S.A.
⟵ 1940	Poinsettia Scarlet	Howard & Smith	U.S.A.
1940	Matador Scarlet-crimson	Dot	Spain
1939	Holstein Crimson	Kordes	Germany
1939	Mme. Henri Guillot Orange-coral-red	Mallerin	France
1938	Saturnia Scarlet	Aicardi	Italy
1938	Sterling Pink	E. G. Hill	U.S.A.
1938	Charlotte E. van Dedem Yellow	Buisman	Holland

YEAR	VARIETY	ORIGINATOR	COUNTRY
1937	Christopher Stone Scarlet	Robinson	England
1937	Golden State Buff-yellow	Meilland	France
1937	Signora Orange-apricot	Aicardi	Italy
1936	Feu Perner-Ducher Yellow	Pernet-Ducher	France
1935	Karen Poulsen Scarlet	Poulsen	Denmark
1935	Eclipse Golden yellow	Nicolas	U.S.A.
1935	Texas Centennial Vermilion-red	Wolfe	U.S.A.
1935	Rochefort Orange	Mallerin	France
1935	Luis Brince Rose-orange	Dot	Spain
1933	Duquesa De Penaranda Orange	Dot	Spain
1929	Julien Potin Primrose yellow	Pernet-Ducher	France
1929	Reveile Dijonnais Cerise	Buatois	U.S.A.
1921	Imperial Potentate Dark rose-pink	Clarke Bros.	U.S.A.
1920	Glenn Dale Lemon white	Van Fleet	U.S.A.
1919	Bloomfield Abundance Salmon-pink	Thomas	U.S.A.
1919	Columbia Rose-pink	E. G. Hill	U.S.A.

ALL-AMERICA ROSE SELECTIONS

All-America Rose Selections, an organization of commercial rose growers, was founded in 1938 for the purpose of testing new roses in all areas of the country and choosing the outstanding varieties for annual awards. All roses are grown and judged for two years in twenty-four official test gardens. The first awards were announced in 1938 and with the exception of 1951, when no rose was found acceptable, awards have been made each year. Announcements are made in June of the year prior to the general distribution of the winners.

YEAR	VARIETY	CLASS	INTRODUCER
1967	Gay Princess Shell pink	Floribunda	Jackson & Perkins
1967	Roman Holiday Red multicolor	Floribunda	Germain's
1967	Bewitched Pink	Hybrid Tea	Germain's
1967	Lucky Lady Pink bi-color	Grandiflora	Armstrong
1966	American Heritage Scarlet	Hybrid Tea	Germain's
	Apricot Nectar Apricot	Floribunda	Jackson & Perkins
	Matterhorn White	Hybrid Tea	Armstrong
1965	Camelot Coral-pink	Grandiflora	Conard-Pyle
	Mister Lincoln Red	Hybrid Tea	Conard-Pyle
1964	Granada Scarlet, nasturtium yellow	Hybrid Tea	Howard Rose Co.
	Saratoga Pure white	Floribunda	Jackson & Perkins
1963	Royal Highness Clear Pink	Hybrid Tea	Conard-Pyle
	Tropicana Orange-red	Hybrid Tea	Jackson & Perkins
1962	Christian Dior Crimson-scarlet	Hybrid Tea	Conard-Pyle
	Golden Slippers Orange-gold	Floribunda	Peterson & Dering
	John S. Armstrong Deep red	Grandiflora	Armstrong
	King's Ransom Chrome yellow	Hybrid Tea	Jackson & Perkins
1961	Duet Bi-color: salmon- pink, orange-red	Hybrid Tea	Armstrong

YEAR	VARIETY	CLASS	INTRODUCER
1961	Pink Parfait Light pink	Grandiflora	Armstrong
1960	Garden Party White	Hybrid Tea	Armstrong
	Fire King Vermilion	Floribunda	Conard-Pyle
	Sarabande Scarlet-orange	Floribunda	Conard-Pyle
1959	Starfire Cherry-red	Grandiflora	Germain's
	Ivory Fashion White	Floribunda	Jackson & Perkins
1958	Fusilier Orange-red	Floribunda	Jackson & Perkins
	Gold Cup Golden yellow	Floribunda	Jackson & Perkins
	White Knight White	Hybrid Tea	Conard-Pyle
1957	Golden Showers Daffodil yellow	Climber	Germain's
	White Bouquet White	Floribunda	Jackson & Perkins
1956	Circus Multicolor	Floribunda	Armstrong
1955	Jiminy Cricket Coral-orange	Floribunda	Jackson & Perkins
	Queen Elizabeth Clear pink	Grandiflora	Germain's
	Tiffany Orchid-pink	Hybrid Tea	Howard Rose Co.
1954	Lilibet Dawn pink	Floribunda	Howard Rose Co.
	Mojave Apricot-orange	Hybrid Tea	Armstrong
1953	Chrysler Imperial Crimson-red	Hybrid Tea	Germain's
	Ma Perkins	Floribunda	Jackson & Perkins
1952	Fred Howard Coral–shell pink Yellow, penciled pink	Hybrid Tea	H & S Nursery

YEAR	VARIETY	CLASS	INTRODUCER
	Vogue Cherry-coral	Floribunda	Jackson & Perkins
	Helen Traubel Apricot-pink	Hybrid Tea	Armstrong
1951	No award was made this year		
1950	Capistrano Pink	Hybrid Tea	Germain's
	Fashion Coral-pink	Floribunda	Jackson & Perkins
	Mission Bells Salmon	Hybrid Tea	Germain's
	Sutter's Gold Golden yellow	Hybrid Tea	Armstrong
1949	Forty-Niner Bi-color: red, yellow	Hybrid Tea	Armstrong
	Tallyho Two-tone pink	Hybrid Tea	Armstrong
1948	Diamond Jubilee Buff	Hybrid Tea	Jackson & Perkins
	High Noon Yellow	Cl. Hybrid Tea	Armstrong
	Nocturne Dark red	Hybrid Tea	Armstrong
	Pinkie Light rose-pink	Floribunda	Armstrong
	San Fernando Currant red	Hybrid Tea	Western Rose Co.
	Taffeta Carmine	Hybrid Tea	Armstrong
1947	Rubaiyat Cerise-red	Hybrid Tea	Jackson & Perkins
1946	Peace Pale gold	Hybrid Tea	Conard-Pyle
1945	Floradora Salmon-pink	Floribunda	Conard-Pyle
	Horace McFarland Buff-pink	Hybrid Tea	Conard-Pyle
	Mirandy Crimson-pink	Hybrid Tea	Armstrong

YEAR	VARIETY	CLASS	INTRODUCER
1944	Fred Edmunds Apricot	Hybrid Tea	Conard-Pyle
	Katharine T. Marshall Deep pink	Hybrid Tea	Jackson & Perkins
	Lowell Thomas Butter yellow	Hybrid Tea	Conard-Pyle
	Mme. Chiang Kai-Shek Light yellow	Hybrid Tea	H & S Nursery
	Mme. Marie Curie Golden yellow	Hybrid Tea	Jackson & Perkins
1943	Grand Duchesse Charlotte Wine red	Hybrid Tea	Conard-Pyle
	Mary Margaret McBride Rose-pink	Hybrid Tea	Jackson & Perkins
1942	Heart's Desire Deep rose-red	Hybrid Tea	H & S Nursery
1941	Apricot Queen Apricot	Hybrid Tea	H & S Nursery
	California Golden yellow	Hybrid Tea	H & S Nursery
	Charlotte Armstrong Cerise-red	Hybrid Tea	Armstrong
1940	Dickson's Red Scarlet-red	Hybrid Tea	Jackson & Perkins
	Flash Oriental red	Cl. Hybrid Tea	Conard-Pyle
	The Chief Salmon-red	Hybrid Tea	Armstrong
	World's Fair Deep red	Floribunda	Jackson & Perkins

12
AMERICAN AND EUROPEAN
ROSE GARDENS

I know a bank whereon the wild thyme blows
Where oxlips and the nodding violet grows
Quite over-canopied with luscious woodbine
With sweet musk roses and with eglantine.
WILLIAM SHAKESPEARE
1564-1616

The public rose gardens listed in this chapter provide an excellent opportunity to see roses growing in their prime, illustrating their best performance in your area. Here you can study the well-established varieties and, in most instances, new introductions. In some gardens you will see roses not yet named that are being test-grown prior to their public debut.

An outstanding public display garden is the one maintained by the Jackson & Perkins Company at its Newark, New York, headquarters. Here in the rolling hill country of upstate New York, just off the New York Thruway and little more than a cool breeze from Lake Ontario, lie seventeen acres of roses. The more than 36,000 plants provide a vista of concentrated loveliness.

The master plan compares favorably with the best rose gardens of America and Europe. The layout is simple but effective. Along a 400-foot central mall are massed formal beds that present a sweeping panorama of brilliant color in red, pink, yellow and white. Forming a focal point at one end are broad patio steps leading to a delightful garden house. Inside, visitors may relax in comfortable chairs and look out at an attractive pool in which a fountain plays a constant stream of cool water. Banked on either side of the long mall are hundreds of thousands of blossoms, each a gem of perfection in form and color.

Along both sides of the garden are several home-size gardens that illustrate effective ways to use roses. There is also a section devoted to experimental roses, many of which will find a place in home gardens throughout America within a few short years. The All-America rose selections have a place of honor and there is also an entire garden devoted to the varieties chosen for the Rose of the Year award.

Anyone interested in roses should make a point of studying the list below and preparing a schedule of rose gardens to visit during the next trip away from home.

Well worth considering is membership in the American Rose Society because of its annual list of Private and Public Rose Gardens. It gives the names and addresses of hundreds of individuals who invite fellow members to visit their gardens, inspect the roses and share experiences in this, the most engrossing hobby of all.

PUBLIC ROSE GARDENS IN UNITED STATES

	APPROXIMATE BLOOMING TIME
Valley Garden Center Rose Test Garden 1809 North 15th Avenue Phoenix, Arizona	March
Berkeley Municipal Rose Garden Euclid Avenue at Bayview Place Berkeley, California	March
Exposition Park Rose Garden Exposition Park 701 State Drive Los Angeles, California	March
State Capitol Grounds Rose Garden Sacramento, California	April
Rose Hills Memorial Park Pageant of Roses Garden 3900 S. Workman Mill Road Whittier, California	March
Elizabeth Park Rose Garden 915 Prospect Avenue West Hartford, Connecticut	June
Shoreham Hotel Rose Garden 2500 Calvert Street, N. W. Washington, D. C.	April
Cape Coral Gardens Cape Coral, Florida	March
Greater Atlanta Rose Garden Piedmont Park Atlanta, Georgia	April

APPROXIMATE BLOOMING TIME

Caldwell Municipal Rose Garden 2101 N. Illinois Avenue Caldwell, Idaho	June
Marquette Park Rose Garden 3540 West 71st Street Chicago, Illinois	June
Sinnissippi Gardens 1300 N. 2nd St., U. S. Rte. 51 Rockford, Illinois	June
Lakeside Rose Garden 1500 Lake Avenue Fort Wayne, Indiana	June
Municipal Rose Garden 236 W. Central Park Avenue Davenport, Iowa	May
Rich Rose Ranch Coldwater, Kansas	May
E. F. A. Reinisch Rose & Rose Test Garden Gage Park Topeka, Kansas	May
Louisiana Agriculture Experiment Station Test Gardens Louisiana State University Baton Rouge, Louisiana	March
Frances Park Memorial Rose Garden 3200 Moore River Drive Lansing, Michigan	June
Minneapolis Municipal Rose Garden 38th & Bryant Avenue, South Minneapolis, Minnesota	June
Municipal Rose Garden Livingston Park Jackson, Mississippi	March
Kansas City Municipal Rose Garden Loose Park 5200 Penn Street Kansas City, Missouri	April

Missouri Botanical Garden 2315 Tower Grove Avenue St. Louis, Missouri	April
Cranford Memorial Rose Garden Brooklyn Botanic Garden 1000 Washington Avenue Brooklyn, New York	June
Niagara Frontier Trial Rose Garden Humboldt Park Buffalo, New York	June
Queens Botanical Garden Flushing, New York	June
Jackson & Perkins Company Newark, New York	June
New York Botanical Garden Bronx Park New York, New York	June
Municipal Rose Garden Maplewood Park Lake Avenue & Driving Park Rochester, New York	June
Dr. E. M. Mills Municipal Rose Garden Thornden Park Ostrom Avenue & University Place Syracuse, New York	June
Sunnyside Rose Garden East 7th Street Charlotte, North Carolina	April
Columbus Park of Roses 4048 Roselea Place Columbus, Ohio	May
Municipal Rose Garden Will Rogers Park 3500 N. W. 36 Street Oklahoma City, Oklahoma	May
Tulsa Municipal Rose Garden 2415 South Rockford Tulsa, Oklahoma	May

APPROXIMATE BLOOMING TIME

International Rose Test Garden 400 S. W. Kingston Avenue Portland, Oregon	June
Hershey Rose Gardens & Arboretum Hershey, Pennsylvania	June
Renziehausen Park Arboretum R.D. #1, Renziehausen Park McKeesport, Pennsylvania	June
Reading Municipal Rose Garden 8th & Washington Street Reading, Pennsylvania	June
Edisto Rose Garden Orangeburg, South Carolina	April
Municipal Rose Garden Warner Park Chattanooga, Tennessee	April
Dallas Garden Center AARS Garden Fair Park Dallas, Texas	March
Municipal Rose Garden Samuell-Grand Park 6200 East Grand Dallas, Texas	March
Houston Municipal Rose Garden Hermann Park Houston, Texas	March
Fort Worth Botanic Garden 3220 Botanic Garden Drive Fort Worth, Texas	March
Tyler Rose Park West Front at Peach Street Tyler, Texas	March
Salt Lake City Municipal Rose Garden 1050 East S. Temple Salt Lake City, Utah	May
Arlington Memorial Rose Garden Bon Air Park Arlington, Virginia	April

APPROXIMATE BLOOMING TIME

Volunteer Park Conservatory 700 North 50th Seattle, Washington	June
Ritter Park Rose Garden McCoy Road Huntington, West Virginia	May
Alfred L. Boerner Botanical Gardens Whitnall Park 5879 South 92nd Street Hales Corners, Wisconsin	June

EUROPEAN ROSE GARDENS

APPROXIMATE BLOOMING TIME

BAGATELLE—France M. Le Conservateur en Chef Chef du Service Technique Les Jardins et Espaces Verts de La Ville de Paris 3 Avenue de La Porte d'Auteuil Paris XVI, France	About 2nd week in June
BADEN-BADEN—Germany Director of Horticulture Attention Herr Rieger Direction of the Parks and Gardens 1 Augustaplatz Baden-Baden, Germany	About 3rd week in June
NATIONAL ROSE SOCIETY—England The National Rose Society Chiswell Green Lane St. Albans, Hertfordshire, England	Last week in June
CITY OF BELFAST—Ireland City of Belfast International Rose Trials Belfast, Ireland	3rd week in June
SPAIN Servicio de Parques y Jardins Parque del Retiro Madrid, Spain	3rd week in May

APPROXIMATE BLOOMING TIME

SWITZERLAND   2nd or 3rd week in June
Concours International de Roses Nouvelles
    Service Des Parcs et Promenades
    Ville de Geneva
120 rue de Lausanne
Geneva, Switzerland
Le President—A. Auberson

HOLLAND   Beginning at end of June and
International Rozen Concours   continuing about 3 weeks
The Hague, Holland

ITALY   3rd week in May
Commune di Roma
Concorso Internazionale Al Premio Roma
Direzione Giardini
Villa Borghese
Rome, Italy

13

JUDGING AND CLASSIFYING ROSES

No one knows
Through what wild centuries
Roves back the Rose.
WALTER DE LA MARE
1873-1956

Should you wish to grow exhibition roses for competition the American Rose Society has an excellent booklet, *The Judging of Roses* by C. H. Lewis, former President of the Society. It will help you learn the basics of rose judging and, equally important, the fine points of the anatomy of a rose.

One of the best ways to learn how to judge varieties is to participate in the Rose Testing Panel conducted by the Jackson & Perkins Company of Newark, New York. Members pay a $10 fee and receive four experimental plants in the Spring. With these plants come full instructions for judging them on a weekly basis. With 100 as the highest possible score, characteristics to be observed are allotted a definite number of points.

SCORING CHARACTERISTICS OF ROSES

(Maximum number of points is given in parentheses)

FOR HYBRID TEA ROSES
Habit (5). Good habit requires upright canes well distributed and later in the season well branched and uniformly balanced.
Vigor (12). Vigor represents growth, good size and continued action through the season. Hardiness is part of vigor, and loss of vitality due to the climate is a fault.
Disease Resistance (8). Represents susceptibility to leaf spot, mildew, rust and other diseases that affect the general health and bloom of the plant.
Floriferousness (12). Floriferousness is scored for quantity or abundant mass of blooms, and also for continuous or repeated blooming through the season.
Stem (5). The stem should be strong enough to support the bloom erectly.

181

Flowers should face the observer. Weak necks are a fault; long cutting stems are an asset.

Foliage (10).   Foliage should not be at too great intervals on the stem or too remote from the bloom. Also should have sufficient size, good texture and good color and be decorative when plant is not in bloom.

Bud Form (11).   Bud form should be judged when the buds start to open and first petals begin to unfold. Bud forms vary—long tapered; ovoid; round.

Flower Form (9).   Blooms should be first judged when one-half open. Flowers should be well centered, petals should unfold evenly, and retain pleasing character until the blooms have aged enough to fall. Full-petaled roses should have nearly a circular outline and center petals of sufficient length to give a uniform balanced appearance.

Substance (9).   Substance is the thickness, firmness, texture and finish of the petals. Blooms that quickly show wilt, burning and shriveling of petals and short life should be severely graded. Petals should also have enough strength to be able to unfold in all weather.

Color-opening (6).   Color should be clear, clean and attractive. A combination of colors should be harmonious, and one which progresses gracefully.

Color-finishing (6).   Complete loss of original color during life of a flower is undesirable. The intensifying of the blue toward unpleasant magenta in reds or pinks is a fault. Unsightly fading of outside petals before bloom is full open is not desirable.

Fragrance (7).   A trace of perfume should have some score. Rich fragrance should be well scored. Roses are not necessarily fragrant at all periods, so if fragrance is not noted, tests should be made throughout the day.

FOR FLORIBUNDAS

Habit (10).   This should provide for the method of branching and general shape of the plants.

Vigor (12).   Vigor represents growth, good size and continued action through the season. Hardiness is part of vigor, and loss of vitality due to the climate is a fault.

Disease Resistance (8).   Represents susceptibility to leaf spot, mildew, rust and other diseases that affect the general health and bloom of the plant. Floribundas should be *very* disease resistant.

Foliage (10).   Foliage should not be at too great intervals on the stem or too remote from the bloom. Also should have sufficient size, good texture and good color and be decorative when plant is not in bloom.

Spray (10).   The spray is the cluster of flowers produced on any basic stem. It should be well balanced, not too crowded or too loose, should face upward and the quantity of blooms should be sufficient to give a massed over-all effect.

Floriferousness (15).   This should include the original burst of flowers, frequency of recurrence and casual flowering in between the heavy bursts of bloom.

Bud Form (4). This represents the size and shape of individual buds when approximately one-third open. Bud forms should be tapered, ovoid or round, as in hybrid teas.

Flower Form (4). Blooms should be first judged when one-half open. Flowers should be well centered, petals should unfold evenly and retain pleasing character until the bloom has aged enough to fall.

Full-petaled roses should have a nearly circular outline and center petals of sufficient length to give a uniform balanced appearance. Semi-double blossoms should be equally as regular in outline.

Since floribundas require less petalage, singles and semi-singles are acceptable on equal basis with doubles and semi-double blooms.

Substance (8). Substance is the thickness, firmness, texture and finish of the petals. Floribunda petals must last in a good clean manner, not burn in sunlight, and drop off cleanly when spent.

Color-opening (8). Refers to bud and one-half open flower. Color should be clear, clean and attractive.

Color-finishing (7). General color of the spray in all stages should be clear, clean and attractive. Faded individual florets in a spray should not be badly off-color, and should not cause the whole spray to be unsightly when all flowers are open.

Fragrance (4). A trace of perfume should have some score; rich fragrance should be well scored.

THE NICOLAS CLASSIFICATION CHART

Benefits of a Classification System. One of the benefits derived from using a classification system is that having once worked out a complete description of a variety you will come to know it intimately and will not likely ever again forget its characteristics. This is especially important in competition where roses must be accurately labeled and judged.

Also, the primary requirement in a rose patent application is a description so complete that it separates the new variety from any other in existence. Such a description has to be minutely detailed since there are many qualities, color and fragrance among them, that could be debatable.

Work on the following classification began some sixty years ago when Monsieur J. Gravereaux, founder of the Roseraie de L'Hay, in France, tried to establish positive identification of rose varieties. Subsequently it was revised by the late Dr. J. H. Nicolas while he was Director of Plant Research for the Jackson & Perkins Company. About the only change since then is the present use of the Ridgway color chart rather than the old Gravereaux color system.

If this chart is followed to the letter the resulting description is comparable to a fingerprint; duplication is practically impossible. In one arbitration case between two nurserymen it was found that two rose varieties were very similar until the genital organs were compared. These differed and when the fruits were developed the variance was so obvious that all doubt disappeared.

Since color is so changeable, the standard time to make color notes is early in the morning as soon as the flower opens. The color should again be noted on the second day, and if it should last that long, on the third day. Otherwise, merely fill in answers to the questions or underscore the words that describe the rose that is to be patented.

DIRECTIONS—Underscore words which describe the rose named; fill in answers to questions.

NAME ....

PARENTAGE—

Seedling or Sport ....
If Seedling—Seed Parent ....
              Pollen Parent ....
If Sport, name parent variety ....

CLASSIFICATION—

Botanic (name strains) ....
Under which it will be in commerce ....

FLOWER

BLOOMING HABIT—

Location where observations were made, date and time of day ....
Blooms Once: Early, midseason, late, profusely, sparsely, has a tendency to give
      few blooms in the Fall.
Recurrent: Continuous, intermittent, Spring and Fall.
Other Habit: ....

BUD—

Size: Very large, large, medium, small.
Form: Short with flat top, long, very long, pointed, urn, ovoid, globular.
      Is it affected by wet weather?................................... How?..............................
      Is it affected by hot weather?................................... How?..............................
Color: When sepals first divide ....
      When petals begin to unfurl ....
      When half blown; inside of petals ....
                    reverse of petals ....

Sepals: Color: Inside.................... Outside....................Smooth edge, serrated, branched, "hood" above bud.

Stand up or curl back; if so, when? ....

Calyx: Color........................ Shape—funnel, pear, apple, other shape........................

Size—large, broad, long, small, slender.

Aspect—smooth, hairy, glandular, mossy.

Odor when rubbed (describe fully) ....

Peduncle: Length—very long, long, medium, short, nested in foliage.

Aspect—smooth, rough, prickly.

Color—light green, medium green, bronzy.

Strength—stiff, erect, weak, bending; heavy, slender.

Opening: Does the bud open well? ....

Is it affected by adverse conditions? ....

BLOOM—

Size: Very large, large, medium, small.

Average size when fully expanded ....

Borne: Singly, several together, in clusters.

If in clusters—pyramidal, rounded, flat or irregular?

Stems: Long, medium, short.

Strong, normal, weak.

Form: When first open—cupped, flat, high center, globular.

Permanence—retains its form to the end; flattens, outer petals curl back; all petals curl quill fashion like a cactus dahlia; like a show dahlia.

Petalage: Single (one row of petals, 4 to 6).

Semi-single (two rows of petals).

Double (full but open center).

Very double (many petals and stamens hidden).

Number of petals under normal conditions ....

Color: (N. B.—Description must be made from a freshly opened bloom cut early in the morning and taken indoors or in shade.) A dominant color can be modified in four different ways, viz:

Lightened by a more luminous color (golden yellow "lightened" with sulphur).

Tinted by a color of same brilliancy (apricot "tinted" with salmon).

Washed by a color more transparent which seems to be superposed (carmine "washed" with sulphur yellow).

Shaded by a color less luminous (pink "shaded" crimson).

Center of flower ....

Outer petals ....

Base of petals (aiglet) ....

Inside of petals ....

Reverse of petals ....

General tonality from a distance ....
Variegations, if any: Bordered (if a line around edge)..
    Margined (if a wide band around edge) ....
    Penciled or veined ....
    Striped ....
    Dotted ....
    Blotched ....
Discoloration: Describe general tonality at end of first day ....
    Second day ....
    Third day ....

PETALS—

Texture: Thick, thin, leathery, soft.
    Is it affected by wet weather?.............................. How?.................................
    Is it affected by hot weather?.............................. How?.................................
Appearance: Inside—shiny, satiny, velvety.
    Outside—Shiny, satiny, velvety.
Form: Round, oval, pointed, notched, scalloped.
Arrangement: Irregular; informal (with "rags" in center); imbricated (regularly
    arranged shinglelike); quartered.
    Petaloids in center; many, few, none, large, small.
Persistence: Drop off cleanly; hang on and dry.
Fragrance: Slight, moderate, strong, none.
    Nature—"Old Rose perfume" (Centifolia), Tea (average Hybrid Tea scent),
    Fruity (Russet apple), Sweetbriar.
    Other fragrance ....
Lastingness: On the plant—very long, long, fair, short.
    As cut flower—very long, long, fair, short.

GENITAL ORGANS—

Stamens, Anthers: Large, medium, small; many, few.
    Color—white, yellow, reddish, brown.
    Arrangement—regular around styles, tucked in calyx or partly so, mixed with
    petaloids.
Stamens, Filaments (threads): Long, medium, short.
    Color—white, yellow, reddish, brown.
Pollen: White, lemon yellow, gold yellow.
Styles: Columnar, bunched, loosely separated, even or uneven length. Short, me-
    dium, long. Thin or heavy.
Stigmas: Color—white, yellow, red, purple, brown or black.
Ovaries: All enclosed in calyx, some protruding from calyx.

FRUIT—

Variety is fertile or sterile with its own pollen?

Form: Round, depressed top, ovoid, round headed, ovoid, flat headed, pear shaped, funnel shaped, gourd shaped, oblong shaped, seeds protruding.
Aspect: Smooth, rough, hairy, prickly, glandular (sticky).
Color at Maturity: Russet brown, yellow, orange, scarlet red, crimson, maroon, black.
Sepals: Caducous (soon falling) or permanent; recurved, curled, straight or spear-shaped.

PLANT

FORM—

Bush, shrub, pillar, rambler, climber.

GROWTH—

Very vigorous, vigorous, medium, stumpy, dwarf, upright, branching, sprawly, compact.

FOLIAGE—

3, 5, 7 leaflets or more? ....
Size: Very large, large, medium, small.
Quantity: Abundant, normal, sparse.
Color—New Foliage: Upper side—light green, normal green, dark green; purple, bronzy.
    Under side ....
Old Foliage: Upper side—light green, normal green, dark green, bronzy, varie-gated, other color.
    Under side ....
Shape: Round, oval, oval pointed, lanceolate.
Texture: Upper side—leathery, glossy, smooth, velvety, flat, corrugated.
    Under side—smooth, rough, velvety.
    Ribs and Veins: Prominent, ordinary, light, impressed.
Edge: Smooth, serrated (saw toothed), undulated.
Serration: Double or single; small, large, sharp, deep.
Leaf Stem: Color—green, reddish, special markings near the axis.
    Under side—smooth, rough, prickles.
Stipules: Long, medium, short. Smooth, serrated, bearded.
Disease Resistance: Susceptible to mildew, blackspot, resistant, immune.

WOOD—

New Wood: Color—light green, dark green, reddish, bronzy, brown.
    Bark: Smooth, rough.
Old Wood: Color—green, brown, black, streaky.
    Bark: Smooth, rough.

THORNS—

(N. B.—Thorns are divided into thorns, prickles and short needles.)

Thorns: Quantity: On main stalks from base—many, ordinary, few, none.
   On laterals from stalk—many, ordinary, few, none.
   Form: Broad base, narrow base, flat base, round base.
      Long, medium, short, straight, hooked downward, hooked upward.
   Color when young: Green, red, green and red, transparent, brown.
   Position: Irregular, in pairs, in sets of three or more.
Prickles: Quantity: On main stalks—many, few, none.
   On laterals—many, few, none.
   Color: Green, brown.
Short Needles: Quantity: On main stalks—many, few, none.
   On laterals—many, few, none.

NOTES: Describe fully other traits or characters or marks of identification ....

14

PLANTING GUIDE

One of the most significant characteristics of the rose is its adaptability. It will grow in all of our fifty states even though temperatures range from an extreme of minus 41 degrees in Caribou, Maine, to 118 degrees F. in Phoenix, Arizona; annual rainfall varies from 59.76 inches in Miami, Florida, to a mere 6.36 inches at Bakersfield, California; and from southern areas that never see snow to Maine where as much as 107.7 inches of snow have fallen in one winter, the ubiquitous rose reigns supreme.

It is frequently stated that roses will thrive in any soil in which vegetables will grow. This is true, but the degree of success depends upon a combination of factors. One of these, the lowest probable annual temperature, is the basis for the Plant Hardiness Zone Map prepared by the U.S. National Arboretum, Department of Agriculture, and the American Horticultural Society. This map is very helpful in determining the need for winter care, whether fall planting is possible and which types of roses may be expected to survive the winter. But, it is a generalized statement that must be used intelligently. Wind, light, moisture, exposure and soil all have an important bearing on the health of roses. All these factors are taken into consideration in the following tabulation of the regional comments from state agricultural experiment stations and the personal experience of home rose gardeners in most of the states.

SEEMING INCONSISTENCIES   In some instances there may seem to be contradictions in the area recommendations for winter care or when plants bloom in a particular city. For instance the state agricultural station may state that winter protection is not needed but an amateur rose grower within the state may declare that rose protection is needed. This may result from a different interpretation of winter protection (that is, amateurs may be using methods other than those given on page 85). Or, it may be that the grower lives at an elevation that results in temperatures colder than those experienced in most parts of the state. If your roses are in a protected area use the earliest planting date given for your area and decide upon winter protection on the same basis. Varying factors can change temperatures or microclimate within a single garden, let alone parts of a city. So the information in the following pages should be regarded as an indication rather than an absolute.

Recommendations of the state agricultural experiment station, or a comparable authority, are given at the beginning of each state listing. Immediately afterward is a listing of recommendations from amateur rose growers who are listed alphabetically by city or town. The key in both instances for the abbreviated information is as follows:

BR—Planting time for bare root roses.
PR—Planting time for potted roses.
WC—Winter care is required. (Whenever WC does not appear, the
area does not require winter care.)

ALABAMA

AUBURN: Henry P. Orr, Alabama Agricultural Experiment Station, BR: Dec., March; PR: any time, with care. Winter protection is not essential except for tree roses. However, since most of the injury done during the winter is by evaporation due to the sun and wind, it may be helpful to give plants some protection. There are several methods for giving roses winter protection. One often used is to clean the ground of dead and diseased leaves and branches after the plants have become thoroughly dormant; remove the mulch if one is used; then, mound soil around the plants to a height of 8 to 10 inches. Care should be taken in removing this soil in the spring. After the danger of freezing has passed, it should be removed slowly on a cloudy or misty day. Many people find that mulched roses are apparently protected adequately by removing the mulch in the fall, allowing the plants to become thoroughly dormant, and then replacing the mulch, increasing the depth immediately around the plants.
    Types of roses: hybrid teas grow well over all the State except possibly in some parts of the southern portion; tea roses, broadly speaking, belong to the southern section. However, they are often used in northern areas when given protection; floribundas are resistant to severe cold and produce many flowers year after year; polyanthas bloom practically all the summer and are good for bedding; hybrid perpetuals are more suited to the northern states than to average Alabama.
    Roses may be planted at any time after they are dormant in the fall until just before growth starts in the spring. However, the earlier in this period they can be planted the better the results will be. Late fall and early winter are the ideal seasons for planting roses.

ALBERTVILLE: Mrs. Charlotte Claybrooke Adams, BR: Jan., Feb.; WC. BAY MINETTE: Mrs. F. P. Eubanks, BR: Nov.-Jan.; WC. BIRMINGHAM: Mrs. H. J. Hooks, BR: Nov.-Feb; PR: any time except June-Aug.; WC. Mrs. W. D. Willett, BR: Feb.-April; PR: March-June. DAPHNE: R. K. Caswell, BR: March-Nov.; PR: same; WC. FLORALA: Mrs. Elizabeth McCune, BR: Nov.; PR: do not plant.

ALASKA

PALMER: Allan D. Mick, Alaska Agricultural Experiment Station, University of Alaska. BR: early June; PR: early June; WC. Few hybrid tea roses survive outdoors in central

Alaska. A few hybrid tea varieties overwinter with mulching in southeast Alaska. Ramblers in favored sites may overwinter in southeast Alaska without special winter care. The hardiest rugosa varieties are common in both Anchorage and Fairbanks.

COLLEGE: Arno Kollis, College Experiment Farm, BR: May 10-June 10; PR: July 1-10, no later); WC. We recommend only rugosas. They need no special winter care, any other type of rose does.

(Ed. note: See experience of Louise Marx in Chapter 6, "Rose Culture for Special Areas.")

ARIZONA

TUSCON: Dr. R. B. Streets, Consulting Rosarian, SW Dist., University of Arizona, BR: Jan.-Feb.; PR: any time, preferably April-May, Sept.-Oct. Temperature and season depend on altitude, and each 1,000 feet (above 3,000) denotes a different climate with different planting and blooming dates. These are comparable to those at equal altitudes in New Mexico; for exmple, Flagstaff, Arizona, equals Santa Fe, New Mexico—7,000 feet.

Our low altitudes have two good blooming seasons: April-May and October-November. There is some bloom all summer, but flowers are of inferior quality, being more subject to heat and wind damage, with fading of color, and, following exposure to dry hot winds, drying of petal edges, etc. Blooms of the more tender varieties which are often wonderful in our coolest blooming weather are worthless in hot weather.

With the long growing season our bushes grow very large. 4 to 7 feet, and should not be pruned low as in the North and East, where frost is apt to dictate how much live wood is present. We need large bushes to shade the ground. With moderate to light pruning, 2 to 3 feet, they live much longer, are sturdier, and will produce much more bloom, with adequate stems.

We have powdery mildew, slight to severe, depending upon the weather. We do not have blackspot, anthracnose or rust.

DOUGLAS: Mrs. W. W. Harsha, BR: end of Oct. to Dec. 10; PR: any time except June through August. MORENCI: Mrs. Garland A. Bull, BR: Feb.-March; PR: March, April; WC. PHOENIX: Mrs. Walter H. Gross, BR: Jan., Feb. WHITERIVER: Vivian Wright, BR: March 1-15; WC.

ARKANSAS

LITTLE ROCK: J. K. Ball, Extension Horticulturist, PR: November, December; BR: November, December. ALMA: Lonniee James, BR: Nov.-Feb.; WC. ARKADELPHIA: W. P. Jones, Jr., BR: March 1-15. BATESVILLE: Katherine B. Grammer; BR: Oct.-Nov., March, April.

CAVE SPRINGS: D. O. Fairley, BR: Oct.-Nov., PR: early spring to June; WC. FAYETTEVILLE: Mrs. J. K. Wheeler, BR: Nov.-Feb.; WC. FORT SMITH: Mrs. Silas J. Baird, BR: March-April; PR: as late as June; WC. HELENA: K. B. Lasswell, BR: Feb. 15; WC. HOT SPRINGS: H. I. Tuttle, BR: Feb. PEEL: Irene B. Sarnow, BR: Sept.-March; PR: April-Sept.

CALIFORNIA

BERKELEY: H. M. Butterfield, Agriculturist Emeritus, University of California, BR: late Dec. thru Jan.; PR: any time after potting or canning in late Jan. Since California has all kinds of climate and growing conditions all that can be given is a general estimate of time for planting bare root roses. The first bare root roses begin to arrive at the retail nurseries in late

December and will usually start to push out new growth during January so most nurseries pot or can roses not sold during late January. These canned roses can be planted when received but best as soon as possible.

An established rose bush which has sent out new growth from September on will often flower on the tips of such growth all through September and scattering as late as December. But the newly planted bush or the pruned rose that sends out growth from January on will likely have its first good crop in the garden in late April or the first week or two in May. Many rose shows have the date set on the assumption that the first good blooms will be expected around May 1.

Most hybrid tea roses have their first important bloom from late April on into May and then flushes of growth may be followed by new crops of bloom. A very good crop of blooms often comes in September but after that any blooms are scattering up into late December in the milder coastal gardens.

Where winters are very mild it is hard to get hybrid teas to go dormant in winter so in many cases the rose bushes are pruned anyway as if they were dormant, preferably in January under normal conditions, except in very cold areas. This winter pruning causes the first crop of bloom to come in late April or early May in the milder parts of California. Where roses are not pruned until the middle of January on hybrid teas, and winters are mild, there may be scattered bloom up to the time of pruning. Susan Louise, which is a seedling of Belle of Portugal, and one of the Hybrid Gigantea roses, may remain almost evergreen in coastal gardens and it is not unusual under these conditions to have flowers scattered all through winter. However, the main flowering comes on the new growth that pushes out in spring, as on most hybrid teas.

CHULA VISTA: Carl Truby, BR: Dec.-Feb.; PR: any time; WC. HOLLYWOOD: George Snow, BR: late Jan. through early Feb.; PR: any time; WC: feeding, pruning in late Nov. OAKDALE: Josephine Salyer, BR: Dec.-March; PR: any time. SANTA ROSA: Harry E. Stebbings, BR: early Jan.

COLORADO

FORT COLLINS: Charles M. Drage, Extension Horticulturist, Colorado State University, BR: March-May; with March-April preferable; PR: March-Sept.; WC. Hybrid tea roses are grown at elevations of 3,500 to 8,500 feet. Soils in Colorado are predominantly alkaline with a pH range of 7.4 to 8.4 quite common. Iron chlorosis is a problem in many rose gardens; however, the rose is the No. 1 garden flower. Infectious rose diseases are not a serious problem, perhaps because of our low humidity. Supplemental water during the growing season is a must; winter watering may be necessary.

ARVADA: May E. Lee, BR: March-April; WC. ASPEN: E. F. Armstrong, BR: April-May; PR: May-July. AURORA: R. L. Kennedy, BR: April-May; PR: May-July; WC. BROOMFIELD: W. P. Coleman, BR: April; PR: June; WC. DELTA: A. F. Fangman, BR: April; WC. DENVER: Walter K. Fleck, BR: March. Dr. A. A. Hermann, BR: March 15-April 15; WC. MALDEN: F. S. Luckey, BR: March-April.

CONNECTICUT

STORRS: Rudy J. Favretti, Extension Home Grounds Specialist, University of Connecticut, BR: April; WC; most definitely. The canes of climbing as well as bush types of roses are often partially or completely killed by winter winds and low temperatures. Make some provision to protect these canes, since the flowering shoots producing spring blossoms develop only from canes grown the previous season. Do not prune any of these vigorous, new canes until spring, when the extent of winter damage can be determined. In late fall, carefully remove branches of less hardy types of climbing roses from their supporting arbor or fence.

Lay them upon the ground and cover with a loose material such as soil, evergreen boughs or straw. Leave the more hardy types on their supports until spring when winter-killed or surplus canes should be removed.

Unprotected canes of garden bush roses, such as hybrid teas, are often partially or entirely winter-killed. If pruned severely in the fall any further injury to canes during the winter could cause their loss to ground level and the death of the plant. To protect further against this danger, hill up 8 to 10 inches of soil around the plant in the fall just before the ground freezes. After freezing starts, mulch the mound with straw, hay, leaves or evergreen boughs. Tie tall canes together to prevent ice or snow damage. Provide additional protection by wrapping the tied canes with evergreen boughs, straw or a burlap snowfence barrier. In the spring, level the soil mound and prune any dead, injured, weak or surplus canes.

BRANFORD: Michael E. Sykes, BR: Sept.-May; WC. DANBURY: Howard R. Sanford, BR: spring and fall; WC. DARIEN: Harry G. Beggs, BR: April. EASTON: George A. Beno, BR: April; PR: May-June; WC. MANCHESTER: Mrs. Alice C. Robert, BR: late April-May; PR: Sept.-June; WC. MIDDLETOWN: Walter J. Zowina, BR: April; WC. SHARON: Miss Elizabeth C. Sawtell, BR: March-April, Oct.-Nov.; WC: first year only. TORRINGTON: Edward Jan-kowski, BR: April; WC. WEST HARTFORD: Mrs. Worthington Mixter, BR: April-May; WC.

DELAWARE

NEWARK: Robert F. Stevens, Delaware Extension Service, University of Delaware, BR: March-April, Oct.-Nov.; PR: May; WC. These dates are for Newark; in southern part of the state, a week earlier.

CLAYMONT: F. Ross Waite, BR: April; WC. DOVER: Mrs. Wm. W. McCoy, BR: March-April; WC. GEORGETOWN: Mrs. Geo. H. Goodge, BR: March; WC. NEWARK: Mrs. W. Francis Lindell, BR: March; WC. NEWARK: Nancy A. Manning, BR: March-April-Nov.; PR: any time; WC. NEW CASTLE: J. Skibicki, BR: April; PR: May. SEAFORD: E. Edwin East, BR: March-May; PR: same; WC. WILMINGTON: G. M. Dillon, BR: Nov.-Dec.-March; PR: April-June. WILMINGTON: Mary Jack Hargis, BR: May; WC. WILMINGTON: Mrs. Victor C. Nah, BR: April-May; PR: March-April; WC.

DISTRICT OF COLUMBIA

WASHINGTON: Mrs. Mae Eleanor Bennett, BR: April-May. WASHINGTON: Charles L. Con-way, BR: March-April; WC.

FLORIDA

GAINESVILLE: S. E. McFadden, Florida Agricultural Experiment Station, BR: South and Central areas when available. North Florida—avoid Oct. and Nov. planting with possibility of repeated freeze injury to new shoots; PR: whenever available from local nurserymen. Stake and tie bushes for wind protection—no other winter protective measures needed for established plants. We recommend wider spacing in planting than in colder regions because rose plants grow larger here.

BR—Planting time for bare root roses. PR—Planting time for potted roses. WC—Winter care is required. (Whenever WC does not appear, the area does not require winter care.)

BOYNTON BEACH: Henry C. Barnes, BR: Oct. BRADENTON: Florence Keniston, BR: spring-fall. COCOA BEACH: Mrs. Fred C. Adams, BR: Oct.; WC. DELAND: Mrs. John D. Masden, BR: Nov.-Dec.; PR: any time in summer. FELLSMERE: Mrs. C. M. Gillespie, BR: Oct.-Feb. FORT LAUDERDALE: Mrs. Wm. C. Knox, BR: Nov.-Jan.; PR: year round. JACKSONVILLE: Mrs. Revon Johnson, BR: Jan. POMPANO BEACH: L. A. Yost, BR: Oct.-Dec.

GEORGIA

ATLANTA: William Y. Klett, BR: Feb.; PR: March-May. ATLANTA: Paul A. Perkins, BR: Dec.-April; PR: May-June; WC. BREMEN: Mrs. J. H. Pritchett, BR: Feb.-March; WC. GRIFFIN: Lewis H. Beck, BR: Nov.-Dec. SAVANNAH: J. M. Jones, BR: Jan.-Feb. ALPHARETTA: Mrs. Mary E. Rogers, BR: March-April; WC: pine, straw mulch. ATHENS: Robert Newton Clark, BR: late Feb., early March; WC.

HAWAII

HONOLULU: Donald P. Watson, University of Hawaii, BR: any month; PR: same; most popular time February. There is great variation in the microclimate within the state. Roses are grown all the way from sea level to 3,000 feet in both arid and high-rainfall areas. The cultural practices vary considerably because of the differences in temperature, humidity, and rainfall. Spraying and pruning are conducted all year round. Garden roses are not a large crop in this tropical environment.

IDAHO

MOSCOW: W. H. Snyder, Agricultural Experiment Station, BR: April-May; PR: April-Oct.; WC. Climatic zones are extremely variable in Idaho; vary from 6a and 6b to Zone 2 hardiness in the high mountain areas. South Idaho is semidesert, requiring irrigation; North Idaho, in the panhandle, has ample moisture. Because of these extremes it is difficult to give general or specific plant material recommendations. There has been limited plant hardiness testing though research projects are now being carried on by our Plant Science Department. Native varieties are to be recommended in areas of extreme cold or drought.

AMERICAN FALLS: Mrs. G. F. Barnard, BR: April; PR: later; WC. BOISE: C. E. Conway, BR: April; PR: same. BOISE: Lorin C. Crockett, BR: April 1 to May 15; PR: April-June. BOISE: Elsie Frahm, BR: April; PR: April 1 through Oct. IDAHO FALLS: Helen M. O'Brien, BR: April; PR: late spring or summer; WC. TWIN FALLS: Mrs. Russell Miller, BR: Feb., early March; PR: May; WC.

ILLINOIS

URBANA: J. B. Gartner, Illinois Agricultural Experiment Station, BR: April 15-June 5 in North; March 15 to May 15 in South; PR: June 1-July 15 in North; May 1-July 1 in South; WC. Due to high winter winds and severe temperature fluctuations, roses do not flourish in Illinois. Even with extreme protection, survival is only fair to good. During the hot humid summers blackspot and other diseases are a common occurrence. Even with these objections, roses are widely grown in Illinois.

ADDISON: Mrs. Donald Cowling, BR: April; WC. ALBION: Mrs. Dennis Hortin, BR: April. ALEDO: Mrs. George O. Hebel, BR: April; WC. ALTON: H. H. Hewitt, BR: early spring, fall; WC. ANNA: Mrs. Berry V. Rife, BR: April, May; WC. ARLINGTON HEIGHTS: G. H. Krohn, BR: April, May; WC. ARLINGTON HEIGHTS: Joseph F. Konen, BR: April; WC. AURORA:

Lloyd R. Doyens, BR: May; WC. AURORA: Robert G. Mickelson, BR: April; WC. AURORA: Henry Ranscher, BR: April; WC. AURORA: Russell Toth, BR: April-May; WC. BERWYN: Joseph Borovec, BR: spring, fall; WC. BERWYN: Martin Knotek, BR: April; WC. BERWYN: Mrs. Wm. Svoboda, BR: April-June; WC. BLOOMINGTON: Mrs. Anne Foreman, BR: April-May. BROOKFIELD: Mrs. Louise M. Orova, BR: April; WC. CAMP POINT: G. E. Jack Dempsey, BR: April-May; PR: May-June; WC. CANTON: Mrs. Gerald Oatman, BR: April-May; WC. CARLINVILLE: Mrs. Charles Barnstable, BR: Depends on weather conditions; WC. CHAMPAIGN: Raymond J. Bulinski, BR: April; WC. CHAMPAIGN: Floyd A. Huff, March-April; WC. CHAMPAIGN: Willis A. Krehin; BR: March-May; WC. CHARLESTON: Mrs. C. P. Young, BR: March; WC. CHICAGO: C. E. Erickson, BR: April-May; WC. CHICAGO: Margaret S. Fay, BR: April; WC. CHICAGO: James K. Wunsch, BR: early April; WC. CHICAGO HEIGHTS: Otis A. Green, BR: early April; WC. COLLINSVILLE: Charles A. Smith, BR: spring; WC. CUBA: Clarence H. Quick, BR: May-June; WC. DECATUR: J. C. McGuire, BR: April; WC. EAST ALTON: Mrs. C. Ray Roberts, BR: Oct.-Nov.-April-May; WC. ELGIN: John H. Kienzle, BR: April-Nov.; WC. ELMHURST: Dr. Walter C. Lading, BR: May; WC. FAIRBURY: Alpha Ferguson, BR: April 15 on; WC. GALVA: Leo White, BR: April; WC. GLENCOE: Fred J. Byington, Jr., BR: early April; WC. HENNING: Clayton Wilcox, BR: April; WC. HIGHLAND PARK: H. F. Borin, BR: April; WC. HOMER: Mrs. Wallace Mills, BR: March-April; WC. HUNTLEY: James T. Venerable, BR: April; WC. LIBERTYVILLE: Robert L. Hoyle, BR: April; WC. MATTOON: A. Richard Boerner, BR: April; WC. MOLINE: Frank DeNess, BR: April-May; WC. POLO: G. J. Lwiker, BR: April; WC. ROCKFORD: Arvid R. Bloom, BR: Mid-April; WC. ROCKFORD: Dr. J. H. Maloney, BR: March-early April; WC. URBANA: G. L. Jordan, BR: April; WC.

INDIANA

LAFAYETTE: E. R. Honeywell, Extension Specialist, Horticulture-Floriculture, Purdue University, BR: March 15-May 1; PR: late April-mid-June; WC. Indiana is a long state from its extreme ends, north to south; and it is subject to many varying environmental conditions. For this reason, it is impossible to state definitely the proper dates to plant roses in Indiana. Normally, the last spring frost dates may vary as much as six weeks throughout the state. I have endeavored to compensate for this in the dates given.

Bedding and cut flower roses: cold bleak winds of winter and dry hot winds of summer are the worst enemies of these roses. For this reason, they should be grown in beds by themselves where they can receive adequate protection, free circulation of air and the best growing conditions.

Indiana has long been known for its wild roses—the roses growing uncultivated along the roadside, on steep banks, along fences and in prairies and swampy areas. They often appear voluntarily where few other plants will thrive. Their ability to grow under so many different situations, their remarkable variation in height and habit of growth and their natural appearance make them ideal for naturalistic plantings. They include: The Meadow rose, *R. blanda* (native to Indiana); the Bristly rose, *R. nitida*; the Swamp rose, *R. palustris*; the Pasture rose, *R. humilis*; the Austrian Brier rose, *R. foetida*; the Sweetbrier rose, *R. rubiginosa*; the Scotch rose, *R. spinosissima*; the Rugosa rose, *R. rugosa*; the Hugonis rose, *R. Hugonis*; the Damask rose, *R. damascena*; the Cabbage or Provence rose, *R. centifolia*; the Wichurian rose, *R. Wichuraiana*; the Prairie rose, *R. setigera*; the Multiflora rose, *R. multiflora*.

ANDERSON: Mrs. Jean Espiggle, BR: April; WC. BEDFORD: Frederick Ernst, BR: Nov. 1-April; PR: spring; WC. BORDEN: Harry A. Jones, BR: April-May; WC. DANVILLE: Mrs. Harry W. Peacock, BR: April 15-May 15; PR: as late as June; WC: very little. EVANSVILLE: Mrs. Rosemary Ritchie, BR: April-Oct.; WC. FORT WAYNE: Herbert Brautzsch, BR: April;

BR—Planting time for bare root roses. PR—Planting time for potted roses. WC—Winter care is required. (Whenever WC does not appear, the area does not require winter care.)

WC. FORT WAYNE: A. J. Ryan, BR: March-April; WC. LAPORTE: Charles Boniface, BR: April 1, Nov. 1; PR: any time in summer; WC. LAPORTE: William J. Ferrier, BR: Sept.-Nov., March-May; WC. LAPORTE: Lawrence Hillborn, BR: April; WC.

IOWA

AMES: Griffith J. Buck, Dept. of Horticulture, Iowa State University, BR: March 2-April 19; PR: May 30-August 1; WC. When planting bare root roses, prepare a liquid starter fertilizer in water. Two tablespoons of 8-8-8, 10-10-10, or another of similar analysis, per gallon of water is suitable. Use 1 or 2 gallons of the liquid fertilizer around each plant.

When preparing to plant a potted rose, put fertilizer into the planting hole. Use 8-8-8, 6-10-4, 5-10-5, 10-10-10 or another with similar analysis. One cupful is sufficient for each plant. Mix the fertilizer into the soil before planting the bush. Failure to mix the fertilizer with soil could result in serious damage to the roots. Dig deeply so that new roots can penetrate without difficulty.

Use a straight edge to determine depth of planting. As with dormant roses the bud union should be 1½ to 2 inches below the soil surface.

ADEL: Raymond Pollock, BR: end of April, first of May; PR: last of May; WC. CEDAR RAPIDS: Mrs. Paul L. Finley, BR: May, June; PR: same. CLINTON: Sanke Hansen, BR: April-Aug.; WC. CONRAD: Mrs. Lyle Olmstead, BR: May, Sept., Oct.; WC. DES MOINES: Larry C. Grove, BR: late April, early May; WC. NEW SHARON: R. Melvin Fleming, BR: early June; WC. PAULLINA: Mrs. Carl Silberstein, BR: May; WC. PERU: Mrs. Wilson J. Datwyler, BR: April, Oct.; PR: May; WC.

KANSAS

MANHATTAN: Charles E. Long, Kansas State University, BR: March-April; PR: March-May; WC. ARRINGTON: Mrs. Clyde Royer, BR: early April; WC. BUFFALO: Otho F. York, BR: April, May; WC. ELLSWORTH: Roy P. Britton, BR: May-June; WC. KENSINGTON: Mrs. B. Hartman, BR: April, May; WC. LEAWOOD: Dr. Wayne A. Wolf, BR: March-April; WC. LEOTI: E. V. Morris, BR: Oct. 15; PR. April 1; WC. WICHITA: O. R. Clapp, BR: March; WC.

KENTUCKY

LEXINGTON: Earl H. New, State Extension Specialist, Ornamental Horticulture, Horticulture Department, University of Kentucky, BR: March-early April; Feb. if early spring; fall if properly protected; PR: late April if properly hardened; fall if properly protected; WC. Spring is usually preferred to fall for planting roses; however, with the protective system suggested in the rose bulletin, Ky. Leaflet 280, fall planting is equally good. Except for occasional winters, most climbers need no protection. In fact, many robust climbing hybrid teas, such as Peace, would flower better if more of the tops froze back to force more severe pruning. After the severe weather in January, 1963, many Peace climbers flowered well after several years of robust growth and few flowers. Hybrid teas and floribundas do need winter protection.

When planting bare-root roses set the graft union at soil level. Many soils are low in phosphorus and potassium as well as nitrogen. For best results, test your soil and add the amounts indicated. The best range for elemental phosphorus is 60-100 pounds per acre and 200-250 pounds for elemental potassium per acre. Add the phosphorus as superphosphate to the rose bed as it is prepared or with the fill soil for single plants. Potash may be added at the same time or later. Both potash and nitrate may be added by spreading them on top of the soil as soon as the plant breaks buds and the soil or mulching material mound or plastic hood is removed. Start feeding potted roses within a week after they are set. Do not lime for roses unless an acidity test shows a pH of 5.5 or less. The best range is 5.5-6.3 pH. Topdress with 2-3 pounds of ammonium nitrate per 1000 square feet when winter protection is removed. In the bluegrass region phosphorus and potassium are abundant in many of the soils. Here, only nitrate applications are needed. After the first application of ammonium nitrate or its equivalent, monthly applications of 1-2 pounds per 1000 square feet may be necessary.

ALBANY: Anne H. Winningham, BR: April 1-15; PR: any time during spring and summer; WC. ASHLAND: William G. Hand, Jr., BR: late March; PR: after May 1; WC. Lester Stemmer, BR: March; WC. DANVILLE: Mrs. Raymond Shewmaker, BR: mid-Nov.; PR: April; WC. LOUISVILLE: Lee E. Cralle, Jr., BR: Nov.; PR: April; WC. James M. Koepper, BR: March-April; PR: April; WC. SALYERSVILLE: Henry R. Mortimer, BR: Nov.; PR: March; WC.

LOUISIANA

BATON ROUGE: W. D. Kimbrough, BR: Jan.-Feb.; PR: any time. Plant adapted varieties; good drainage essential; a loose soil containing organic matter; full sun if possible; fertilizer properly used; irrigate during dry periods; spray with proper fungicide once a week especially to control blackspot. Do not overcut blooms, especially on young plants. Prune to 18 to 20 inches in January or February.

ALEXANDRIA: Mrs. Richard East, BR: Nov.-March; PR: any time; WC. BATON ROUGE: J. W. Hathorn, BR: Dec.-Jan.; PR: Feb.-March. Clara Tucner, BR: March-April; PR: Jan.-Feb.; WC. BOSSIER CITY: George E. Bethke, BR: Dec.-Feb.; PR: March-May; WC. BRUSLY: Curtis A. Dupuy, BR: March-May; PR: any time except Dec.-Jan.; WC. BUNKIE: Miss Mary M. Haas, BR: Dec. CHATHAM: Mrs. G. A. Moore, BR: Nov.-Dec.; PR: Jan.-Feb.; WC. LAKE PROVIDENCE: John O. Nelson, BR: Nov.-Dec.; PR: any time; WC. MAPLEWOOD: Mrs. T. H. Nixon, BR: Feb., March.

MAINE

ORONO: Lyle Littlefield, University of Maine, BR: April-May; PR: April-July; WC. Surest method of winter protection would be to bury plants in a trench (well drained site) for the winter. This is done on many estates. Recommend planting more of the hardy shrub types, especially rugosa.

AUBURN: Morris L. Ellingwood, BR: late April-early June; PR: April, early June; WC. NORTH BATH: Mrs. Edwin A. Hemingway, BR: April-May; WC. BETHEL: Gerry Brooks, BR: late May; WC. BOWDOINHAM: Eara A. Stevens, BR: end of April; WC. CALAIS: Percy E. Jackman, BR: mid-May; PR: mid-May; WC. CAPE NEDDICK: Mrs. Peter Mawn, BR: April 20-30; PR: May or June; WC. ROCKLAND: Miles Sawyer, BR: April; PR: May and June; WC. SOUTH PARIS: R. Decato, BR: May-June; PR: same; WC.

MARYLAND

COLLEGE PARK: Prof. Conrad B. Link, University of Maryland, BR: Oct.-Nov.; PR: March to Nov. (could be any season if properly planted). No winter protection is needed except for roses planted as late as December, and in the higher elevations such as Hagerstown and west.

BR—Planting time for bare root roses. PR—Planting time for potted roses. WC—Winter care is required. (Whenever WC does not appear, the area does not require winter care.)

Maryland's climate varies widely with a growing season of 130-140 days in the western part to 200 days on lower eastern shore. Mid portion of state, 170-180 days.

It is advisable to plant roses in the fall when soil and air conditions are most favorable. Frequently the soil is so wet in the spring that it is not possible to work it conveniently and plant when the bushes arrive. Fall planting is most easily done after the plants are dormant but before freezing weather sets in. This is usually during November. Spring planting should be done as early as possible, preferably from early March to early April. If the weather is very cool it is advisable to mound the soil around the base of the canes as in fall planting. The bud union should be at or slightly below the soil level.

For fall planted roses the soil should be mounded to 6 to 10 inches around the base of the canes for protection over the winter. In the colder sections of the state or where planting may not be done until in December, this soil mound should be supplemented with a mulch of leaves or straw before severe freezes are likely to occur. The canes of newly planted roses in the spring may be covered with moist burlap, newspaper or other material to keep them from drying out until the roots become established. Whatever the material used, it should be removed as soon as the buds start to grow. Plants growing in pots are available through the spring and summer. These are useful to fill in vacant spaces where it has not been possible to plant early in the season. Pot grown plants are better for late planting than dormant plants.

BALTIMORE: Virginia H. Whitridge, BR: March-Nov.; WC. BETHESDA: Frederick K. Hayes, BR: March and Sept. ELLICOTT CITY: Mrs. Charles F. Phillips, Jr., BR: April 15-Sept. 15; PR: any time; WC: new-yes; old-no.

MASSACHUSETTS

AMHERST: Alfred W. Boicourt, University of Massachusetts, BR: April 20 to mid-June; Oct. thru Nov. is possible in many areas; PR: May 15-June 30; WC. Many areas of the state are bothered by wide fluctuation in temperature during the winter months. Hilling with soil is advisable; mulching is also advisable but seldom practiced except by rosarians.

Dry spells in midseason cause considerable damage to late-planted roses, either bare roots or canned.

AGAWAM: Mrs. Gino Rossi, BR: May or June; WC. ARLINGTON: Min Sickles, BR: May and Oct.; WC. BELMONT: Mrs. Reo J. Marcotti, BR: late April or early May; WC. BOSTON: Mrs. Ida Perkins, BR: early spring or fall; WC. BUZZARDS BAY: Mrs. Esther G. Clark, BR: May; WC. CANTON: Kenneth Reed, BR: May and Oct.; WC. DEDHAM: Mrs. Ethel L. Martin, BR: late April; WC. FRAMINGHAM: J. J. Slomski, BR: May or Oct.; WC. HANOVER: Miss Helen Morton, BR: April or early May; WC. HUDSON: John M. W. Sargent, BR: April; WC. LEE: David Hellstrom, BR: April; WC. LOWELL: Miss Priscilla Jensen, BR: May; WC. MARSHFIELD: Mrs. Donald M. Flocke, BR: April and May; WC. MEDFORD: Vincent J. Rivela, BR: Oct. NEWTON CENTER: Eli Shapiro, BR: March. NORTH ATTLEBORO: Georgina L. Griswold, BR: May; WC. PITTSFIELD: Eva May Fish, BR: April and Oct.; WC. RAYN-HAM: Andrew Plentus, BR: late April-May; PR: any time before Aug. 1; WC. SPRINGFIELD: John H. Bunt, Jr., BR: May-June; WC. T. S. Rowe, BR: April and Nov.; WC. WAKEFIELD: John Brown, BR: late April-early May; PR: May and June; WC. George J. Jung, BR: April; WC. WATERTOWN: Earl Sawyer, BR: April; WC. WINTHROP: Adelaide Vigliane, BR: Nov.

MICHIGAN

EAST LANSING: Richard F. Stinson, Assoc. Prof. Hortl., Michigan Agricultural Experiment Station, Michigan State University, BR: first week in April. Fall not recommended; PR: early spring to mid-Oct.; WC. In the Detroit area planting could be one week earlier than above; in upper peninsula and upper lower peninsula, one to two weeks later.

Flowering in lower Michigan would be about one week earlier than the above date—for central Michigan—and about one to two weeks later for the upper peninsula and upper part of the lower peninsula.

In the Detroit area roses are often successfully wintered by covering only with pea hampers. In central Michigan hilling and the application of a straw mulch after the soil is frozen is essential. Along Lake Michigan and in the northern part of the state snowfall is usually so heavy that the plants are well protected from cold-damage—but an open winter with low temperatures can be very damaging.

Soil conditions vary so much in the state, often even within a matter of a few hundred yards that only the most general recommendations can be made.

ADRIAN: Mrs. Victor Agnew, BR: June. AKRON: Milton J. Bender, BR: Nov. and May; WC. ALGONAC: Miss Wilda Bradley, BR: April-May; WC. ALLEGAN: Mrs. Lester Cornell, BR: May; PR: May-June; WC. ALLEN PARK: Mrs. Marie Sayyae, BR: May; WC. Vincent R. Stitz, BR: April or May; WC. ANN ARBOR: W. A. Stacey, BR: Oct. or May; WC. BATTLE CREEK: Mr. and Mrs. Ray J. Abbot, BR: April; WC. BAY CITY: Michael Morin, BR: April-May; WC. BIRMINGHAM: Mrs. C. F. Meanwell, BR: April and Oct.; WC. CASSOPOLIS: Mrs. H. Simmons, BR: May; WC. DEARBORN: Mr. and Mrs. F. Cain, BR: April-June; WC. Mrs. Joseph Miklosky, BR: May; WC. DETROIT: Anne Applebaum, BR: May and June. Mrs. Jack Callender, BR: May and June, Sept. and Oct.; WC. Ruby Renette, BR: April-May; WC. Frances E. Schornack, BR: March-April. EAST LANSING: Mrs. William Dovorn, BR: April and Oct.; WC. Earl C. Richardson, BR: May and June; WC. FLINT: Archie K. Higgins, BR: late April or early May and Oct.; PR: any time; WC. Mrs. Merle G. Penz, Sr., BR: April; WC. Gail S. Smith, BR: early May; WC. FLUSHING: Cecil L. Meadows, BR: April or Oct.; WC. GARDEN CITY: Arlo Glenn, BR: April or May; WC. GRAND RAPIDS: Norman S. Byram, BR: May; PR: May; WC. Mrs. John Rozsa, BR: April 1 and Nov. 1; WC. GROSSE POINTE: Elmore W. Frank, BR: April; WC. Mr. James H. Doherty, BR: April and May; WC. HARPER WOODS: Mrs. J. Lenzing, BR: fall or spring (mostly spring); WC. HAZEL PARK: Mr. and Mrs. Chas. Kunze, Sr., BR: spring and fall; WC. JACKSON: Harry E. Burgess, BR: April 15-20; WC. LAKE CITY: Mrs. Walter Hunt, BR: May; WC. MADISON HEIGHTS: Robert F. Luther, BR: April-June. OAK PARK: Dr. Donald L. Kitai, BR: April and May; WC. OWOSSO: J. L. Dingwalld, BR: Oct., WC. PONTIAC: Thomas Horwitz, BR: April-Oct.; WC. ROMEO: Mrs. Betty Guepper, BR: spring; WC. ROSEVILLE: Roy F. French, BR: April and May; WC. ST. CLAIR SHORES: Mrs. Lyle G. Campbell, BR: April or May; WC. ST. JOSEPH: Mrs. Martin Howard, BR: early spring; WC. SCOTTS: Beatrice E. Statler, BR: April or May; PR: any time April-Oct.; WC. SOUTHFIELD: Amos Crittenden, BR: May or June; WC. SOUTHGATE: Mrs. Victor J. Hurych, BR: Oct.; WC. TRAVERSE CITY: Miss Mary A. Jelinek, BR: April-May; WC. WAYNE: Mrs. Margaret Hayden, BR: Oct.; WC.

MINNESOTA

ST. PAUL: Prof. Leon C. Snyder, University of Minnesota, BR: April 10-May 20; PR: May 1-July 31; WC. Temperatures in Minnesota often drop to minus 50° F. in northern parts of the state. Temperatures of minus 30° F. are not uncommon in southern Minnesota. Summers are usually warm and dry. Normal winter protection is not adequate. Trenching and leaf cover to a depth of 18 to 24 inches is recommended.

ADAMS: Carl J. Winkels, BR: May; PR: June-July; WC. COLDSPRING: W. Conrad, BR: May; PR: May-June; WC. DULUTH: Axel Eikholm, BR: early June; PR: May; WC. S. C. Sorenson, BR: May 1; WC. MINNEAPOLIS: H. C. Chamberlin, BR: early May; WC. Donald S. Jepsen, BR: April; WC. NORTH ANOKA: Don Lindgren, BR: April-June; WC.

BR—Planting time for bare root roses. PR—Planting time for potted roses. WC—Winter care is required. (Whenever WC does not appear, the area does not require winter care.)

NORTH ST. PAUL: Mrs. L. P. Gruber, BR: April or May; PR: as late as July; WC. SOUTH ST. PAUL: Mrs. Abe Rosenbaum, BR: May, June and Oct.; PR: May and June; WC.

MISSISSIPPI

STARKSVILLE: W. C. Gordon, Agricultural Experiment Station, Mississippi State College, BR: Nov. thru Feb.; PR: Nov. thru April; WC. There is much discussion among rose growers as to when to set bare root plants in Mississippi, fall or spring. Good results have been gained by planting in both seasons, if plots are given proper cultivation. But usually Mississippi soils are not truly cold enough to set dormant plants until late winter or early spring. The bud union should be set about an inch above ground level.

Having your soil tested before you apply any fertilizer is recommended. Soil testing services are available through local cooperative extension service agents. Although the specific amount of fertilizer to use should be based on results of a soil test, most garden soil in Mississippi benefits from three applications of a 9-12-12 fertilizer at the rate of 3 pounds to each 100 square feet of bed. Make the first application in March, the second in June and the last in August.

Prune roses each year between February 20 and March 15.

Space hybrid teas, grandifloras and polyanthas 3 feet by 3 feet in the bed. Space floribundas 4 feet by 4 feet, miniature roses 1 foot apart; hybrid perpetuals 5 feet apart and climbers at least 10 feet apart.

BAY SAINT LOUIS: Mrs. Axel Hansen, BR: Nov.-Feb.; PR: Winter months; WC. BILOXI: Vera K. Russell, BR: Nov. and Jan. or Feb.; PR: late Feb. or March; WC. JACKSON: A. Ray Tillman, BR: Jan. MERIDIAN: Robert E. Harrison, BR: Nov. and Dec.; WC. POPLARVILLE: Mrs. L. C. Rouse, BR: Nov. and Dec. RUTH: Mrs. Lowrey Burn, BR: Sept. and March; PR: March and April; WC. SAUCIER: Margaret Warden, BR: Dec. and Feb.-April; PR: Nov.-May. SHANNON: Mrs. Edwin Robbins, BR: March or earlier; PR: as late as June; WC. SUMMIT: Mrs. David Hutchison, BR: Jan. 15-March 1; PR: Jan.-March; WC.

MISSOURI

COLUMBIA: Charles M. Sacamano, University of Missouri, BR: March-April; PR: March thru Sept.; WC.

ADRIAN: Mrs. Vernon W. Welch, BR: April; WC. CLAYTON: Harry M. White, BR: April or late fall; WC. FLORISSANT: Mrs. Donna M. Whitaker, BR: April-May, Sept.-Oct.; WC. JOPLIN: Martha Siebenthaler, BR: mid-May-June; PR: mid-May; WC. KANSAS CITY: Mrs. John D. Plumb, BR: March; WC. KIRKWOOD: Robert L. Young, Jr., BR: March; WC. OREGON: Mrs. John G. Bowes, BR: April; PR: through May; WC. ST. LOUIS: J. C. Ballinger, BR: March-April. WEBSTER GROVES: Frank R. McMath, BR: March and April; WC.

MONTANA

BOZEMAN: Orville W. McCarmer, Horticultural Specialist, Montana State University, BR: mid-April to mid-May; PR: to July 1st; WC. Our climatic conditions are such that we can grow hybrid teas and floribundas, plus various shrub roses and the Paul's Scarlet climber, only in the warmer areas. Rugosas are used throughout the state. In all areas we suffer heavy losses from winterkill, especially on hybrid teas and floribundas, sometimes in spite of winter protective measures. Our principal diseases are powdery mildew and rust; insects include aphids, thrips, leafhoppers, spider mites and petal-eating earwigs. *R. alba* and *R. turkestanica* are used as substitutes for multiflora in hedges. Harrison's Yellow and Persian Yellow are very good shrub roses for our state.

BIG TIMBER: Pearl Miller. BR: late Aril-early May; WC. BILLINGS: Mrs. Rex Barkhaff, BR: mid-April thru May; PR: May and June; WC. ROZEMAN: Mrs. B. L. Dusenberry, Jr., BR: late April and May; PR: late April-June; WC. HELENA: Burt C. Jensen, BR: April; PR: March; WC. SHERIDAN: Mrs. Harry L. Kurfiss, BR: late April; WC. THOMPSON FALLS: Mrs. Hugh Hearing, BR: April 18-May 5; PR: May 1-June 15; WC. TOSTON: Mrs. Walter F. Rauser, BR: May-June; PR: mid-June; WC.

NEBRASKA

LINCOLN: Wayne C. Whitney, Extension Horticulturist, University of Nebraska, BR: late March to early May; PR: late May to Aug.; WC.

AUBURN: Carl A. Nordlund, BR: May and June; WC. BERWYN: Ernest Rapp, BR: May; WC. BRAINARD: R. J. Horacek, BR: early May; WC. GRANT: Mrs. Harry Saum, BR: May; WC. LEXINGTON: Lester Hildenbrandt, BR: April 15 to end of May; PR: May-June; WC.

NEVADA

RENO: Ray E. Ely, Assoc. Dir., Nevada Agricultural Experiment Station, BR: late March-early April; PR: May thru Sept.; WC. The above comments are for Northern Nevada only.
Fall planting is not recommended generally because the field-grown roses do not go dormant early enough. Recommend only spring planting for bare root roses.

BOULDER CITY: Mrs. H. S. Curtis, BR: Jan.-Feb.; PR: Jan.-Feb., Oct.-Nov. CARSON CITY: Peter J. Herlan, BR: March 15-21; PR: Sept.-Oct.; WC. HAWTHORNE: Johnnie W. Payne, BR: late March-early April; PR: any time; WC. LAS VEGAS: Marie O'Day Rhodes, BR: Jan. or Feb.; PR any time; some WC. RENO: Marion E. Cazier, BR: Feb.-April; PR: May-Sept.; WC. SPARKS: Mrs. Ernest Perry, BR: Feb.-March; PR: any time except mid-winter, mid-summer; WC. WINNEMUCCA: Frayce Campbell Lamb, BR: May; WC.

NEW HAMPSHIRE

DURHAM: Radcliffe B. Pike, University of New Hampshire, BR: spring only. April to early May; PR: late May and June; WC. Winter survival precarious at best unless heavily covered. Only certain method for year after year survival is to dig up and bury horizontally a foot or more deep in late November and dig up and replant in April. This is probably less labor than hilling up. I carried 50 hybrid teas this way for ten years with no winter losses.

CLAREMONT: Harold P. Fletcher, BR: April; WC. CONTOOCOOK: H. C. Albin, BR: late April-early May; WC. EXETER: Mr. and Mrs. Corning Benson, BR: May; PR: May 15; WC. FRANKLIN: Mrs. Sears Fuller, BR: April 19-26; WC. LEBANON: Mrs. F. O. Whitcomb, BR: May; WC. NASHUA: Miriam Dionne, BR: mid-April to early June; PR: June; WC. PORTS-MOUTH: Mildred Packard, BR: June 1, PR: same; WC.

NEW JERSEY

NEW BRUNSWICK: Donald B. Lacy, Home Horticulture Extension Specialist, College of Agriculture and Environmental Science, Rutgers University, BR: March-1st week of April, late

---

BR—Planting time for bare root roses. PR—Planting time for potted roses. WC—Winter care is required. (Whenever WC does ńot appear, the area does not require winter care.)

Nov. PR: May thru Oct.; WC. Many dealers prefer to sell container roses now. The customer is sure of a live plant of the desired variety at planting time and is usually willing to pay more for a container rose. The long selling season is a real advantage for the dealer.

ATLANTIC CITY: Dr. Ralph J. Nigro, BR: April. BAYONNE: Frank P. Effinberger, BR: March; WC. Mrs. F. Stenson, BR: April or Nov.; PR: May; WC. BERGENFIELD: Ed Kinnaugh, BR: Oct. or April. CRANFORD: Thomas S. Capron, BR: March-April; WC. DEMAREST: William J. Gruby, BR: March. DOVER: Warren M. Apgar, BR: April. DUMONT: Frank Vira, BR: Oct. EAST BRUNSWICK: James Larrousse, BR: May, PR: May-June; WC. FLEMINGTON: Percy Hewitt, BR: March 20; PR: April-May; WC. HADDONFIELD: Mrs. Claire A. Harden, BR: April. JERSEY CITY: Mrs. Genevieve Grabowski, BR: early April or late Oct. LEBANON: Roy O. Hendrickson, BR: April; WC. LITTLE FALLS: Mrs. Harold Harding, BR:. Nov. and April; WC. MILLVILLE: V. P. Zatkalik, BR: mid-March; WC. NUTLEY: Mr. Stephen Zadoyko, BR: May; WC. PENNSAUKEN: F. J. Engel, BR: March-April, Oct.-Nov. PERTH AMBOY: John E. Sullivan, BR: Sept. RIDGEWOOD: Mrs. Francis J. Walsh, BR: May and Nov.; WC.

NEW MEXICO

UNIVERSITY PARK: Fred B. Widmoyer, Department of Horticulture, New Mexico State University, BR: early Feb.; PR: year round. In southern part of the state bare-root roses can be planted whenever they can be obtained; in the northern areas, in March and April. Mulching may prove beneficial to prevent desiccation during cold windy weather. Iron chlorosis is a problem because of high calcium and sodium content. Sprays of iron sulfate or soil applications of sulfasoil easily control the problem. Our soils are low in organic matter. If New Mexico rose growers spent the amount of money for organic matter that rose growers in other areas spend on disease control, they would produce better roses. Nitrogen applications spaced at biweekly intervals and at lower levels are useful.

ALBUQUERQUE: Mrs. Dale J. Bellamah, BR: April-May; PR: April-Oct.; WC. BELEN: Mrs. G. A. Lovett, BR: March-early April; PR: May thru Aug.; minimum WC. CARLSBAD: Charles W. Lewis, Jr., BR: late March; PR: same; WC. DORA: Mrs. Garth Bielss, BR: March; PR: late April-early May; WC. LAS CRUCES: Mrs. Bert LaDriere, BR: Dec.-Feb.; PR: any time; WC. LAS VEGA: Mrs. Iva Zimmerman, BR: April; WC.

NEW YORK

ITHACA: Prof. A. M. S. Pridham, Cornell University, BR: April 15-May 15, Oct. 15-Nov. 15 PR: late May to fall; WC. In the spring loosen and remove mound soil when lawns green up—unless killing frosts are predicted for the week ahead. Prune out dead wood. Diseased foliage should be removed in fall and spring as well as during the growing season. At Cornell we plant in both the fall and spring but it is important to protect roses planted in November.

ADAMS: Mrs. Elsie H. Bechtel, BR: May; WC. Mrs. H. E. Richardson, BR: Oct. and late April; WC. AKRON: Mr. Dorsey Bailey, BR: late April or early May; WC. ALBANY: Benjamin B. Reed, BR: April-Oct.; WC. Townsend Rich, BR: April; WC. ALBION: W. D. Enzie, BR: April-May; WC. ALLEGANY: Donald G. Holmes, BR: Oct. and April; WC. ALTAMONT: H. J. Hughes, Jr., BR: April-May; WC. ANCRAM: Mrs. R. G. Block, BR: May; WC. ANGOLA: Eugene Bower, BR: April-May; WC. ARCADE: Harry S. Douglass, BR: late April or early May; WC. ARMONK: Mrs. Cleve W. Clark, BR: May; WC. ASTORIA: Elizabeth M. Stein, BR: May or Sept.; WC. AUBURN: Ardis M. McCarty, BR: April-May; WC. John Quiggle, BR: May, June, Sept.; WC. BALDWIN: Mrs. A. D. Schnebbe, BR: April-May. BELLEROSE: Shirley S. Maslow, BR: April; WC. BELLPORT: Mrs. John Conway, BR: fall; WC. BETHPAGE: James W. Ackell, BR: fall; WC. Mrs. Eleanor Clark, BR: May; WC.

BLISS: Mrs. Joseph Biscaro, BR: May and June; WC. BOLIVAR: H. J. Loop, BR: May; WC. BRONXVILLE: Mrs. E. E. Quantrell, BR: Oct. BROOKLYN: Alfred Palumbo, BR: April; WC. CAMDEN: O. Leonardson, BR: April and May; PR: June and July; WC. CAMILLUS: Mrs. John F. Lehman; BR: May; WC. CATSKILL: A. E. Larsen, BR: April; WC. CENTEREACH: Clarence Powell, BR: May; WC. CENTRAL SQUARE: Harlan C. Shaw, BR: April or May; WC. DELMAR: Mrs. Edgar L. Potter, BR: May; WC. ELMHURST: Thomas Liguori, BR: March or Nov. FAYETTEVILLE: James R. Mitscher, BR: April or early May; WC. GLENS FALLS: George Teague, BR: Nov. and May; WC. GREAT NECK: Thomas C. Houts, BR: end of March. GROTON: Wayland G. Rice, BR: Oct. and Nov.; WC. HANNIBAL: Beverly Barry, BR: late April, early May; WC. HEMPSTEAD: Mrs. M. Mandsley, BR: April. HERKIMER: Mr. and Mrs. Donald F. Morse, BR: May and June; WC. HORNELL: Wm. J. Nary, BR: April or Oct.; WC. ITHACA: Mrs. John M. Liddel, BR: fall; WC. D. T. Kresge, BR: May; WC. JAMESTOWN: Lawrence A. Dorler, BR: April-June; WC. JERICHO: Nathan J. Ackerman, BR: April-May, Sept.-Oct.; WC. KENMORE: Mrs. A. A. Gorney, BR: early May; WC. LARCHMONT: Mrs. Leroy Lewis, BR: Nov. LAURELTON: Mrs. D. Fox, BR: Oct. and April. LEVITTOWN: William H. Sechrengost, BR: May-June and Oct.; WC. LINDENHURST: Mrs. S. Abrahamsen, BR: March or Oct.; WC. LYNBROOK: Ida Dianne Cantor, BR: April-May. MASAPEQUA: Jasper J. Jenkins, BR: Oct.; WC. MECHANICVILLE: Phyllis M. Tate, BR: early June and late Oct.; WC. MIDDLESEX: Howard Fischer, BR: late May-early June; PR: July; WC. MIDDLE VILLAGE: A. Castoria, BR: April-June; WC. MINEOLA: Mrs. Henri Jourdain, BR: early April. MONROE: Mrs. Guy H. Peifer, BR: early May; WC. MONSEY: William C. Seidel, BR: spring. MONTROSE: Benjamin F. Pattison, BR: Sept.; WC. NEWFIELD: Mrs. Howard A. Bingham, BR: May; WC. NICHOLS: Myron D. Albro, BR: late April and early May; WC. NORTH SYRACUSE: Howard L. Stevens, BR: April-May; WC. NORTH TONAWANDA: Mrs. Joseph Wilezak, BR: May-June. ONTARIO: Mrs. Norman E. Harris, BR: June-Aug., late Oct.; WC. ORCHARD PARK: Mrs. Harold Erickson, BR: late April. PELHAM: Mrs. John O'Gorman, BR: Nov. and late March; WC. ROCHESTER: Leo Roach, BR: Nov.-Dec., late March-April; WC. ROME: Dr. and Mrs. William Tracy, BR: Nov.; WC. SKANEATELES: Vera W. Howard, BR: April and Oct. SNYDER: Dr. R. Gartler, BR: April-May; PR: before July 1. WASHINGTON: Mrs. John J. Floherty, BR: Oct.-Nov.

NORTH CAROLINA

RALEIGH: F. D. Cochran, North Carolina Experiment Station, BR: Feb.-March; PR: Feb.-May; WC. The above dates are generally recommended, however, plants may be set during late fall and winter as soon as available. In these cases they should be well protected above the crotches by a mound of soil.

ASHEVILLE: Capt. E. E. Saunders, BR: April; WC. BROWN SUMMIT: Mrs. Allen J. Brown, BR: Nov.; PR: late March, early April; WC. CARY: Michael J. Kollar, BR: March; PR: any time; WC. CHARLOTTE: R. N. Hughes, BR: late March; PR: late March to Oct. 15; WC. FAYETTEVILLE: Mrs. W. E. Hollingsworth, BR: March; WC. S. G. Rackley, BR: March; PR: March and April; WC. A. Glenn Newberry, BR: early April; WC. GRAHAM: K. W. Donaldson, BR: March-May; WC.

NORTH DAKOTA

FARGO: Donald C. Hoag, North Dakota State University, BR: mid-April thru May; PR: May-June; WC. Mounding bare root roses with soil at planting time is essential because of low humidity and rapid and extreme temperature fluctuations. For winter care, roses should be mounded or covered with leaves or vermiculite in very late October or early November.

BR—Planting time for bare root roses. PR—Planting time for potted roses. WC—Winter care is required. (Whenever WC does not appear, the area does not require winter care.)

206 The Magic World of Roses

ANTLER: Mrs. Donald R. Floyd, BR: May; PR: May; WC. BOWMAN: Olaf Nielson, BR: May; WC. FARGO: Mrs. F. D. Bergstrom, BR: May 20; PR: May 30 to June 15; WC. GRAND FORKS: Wallace W. Nelson, BR: June; WC.

OHIO

COLUMBUS: L. C. Chadwick, Department of Horticulture, Ohio State University, BR: early April; PR: any time during growing season; WC. Planting period for bare root roses varies greatly: fall, October and November; spring, late March to mid-May.

Winter care: our practice is to replenish a ground corncob mulch to a depth of about 4 inches each fall. No hilling is practiced. Hilling is practiced by many rose growers in the state.

ATTICA: Mrs. Velma I. Weaver, BR: late March, early April; PR: June; WC. BEDFORD: Mrs. Viola L. Ridgway, BR: late April, early May; WC. BLUFFTON: H. W. Berky, BR: April; WC. CADIZ: Mrs. Ralph Hilbert, BR: April; WC. CAMBRIDGE: Mr. and Mrs. Paul D., Secrist, BR: May; WC. CANTON: Mrs. W. H. Doty, BR: April; WC: CHILLICOTHE: Mrs. Robert Newton; BR: April; WC. CINCINNATI: Raymond C. Brossart, BR: Oct. or April; WC. Raymond Clubb, BR: late March, early April; WC. Mrs. W. R. Dally, BR: April; PR: May. Mrs. Alton Durham, BR: April-June; WC. CLEVELAND: John Paul Bell; BR: April-May. COLUMBUS: Mrs. David W. Parker, BR: April-May; WC. CRESTLINE: Milo Wachs, BR: April; WC. DAYTON: Blair E. Caplinger, BR: April-June, Sept.-Oct.; WC. Mrs. W. Z. Zimmerman, BR: fall; WC. Mrs. M. Christine Clark, BR: March and Nov. Mrs. E. W. Vossler, BR: May-June; WC. FINDLAY: Richard G. Robinette, BR: April; WC. GALLIPOLIS: Mrs. Roma Northup; BR: April and Sept.; WC. HAMILTON: Clinton Dunlap; BR: March; WC. HILLSBORO: Mr. and Mrs. Elmer C. Vogel, BR: May and Oct.; WC. LIMA: Mrs. John Albert, Jr., BR: Nov. and March; WC. LOVELAND: Mary Holwadel, BR: April; WC. MAGNOLIA: Mrs. Bernice Bordner, BR: April; WC. MARION: Mrs. Richard E. Lawrence, BR: March and Sept.; WC. MEDINA: Mrs. Delbert Packard, BR: March; WC. MILLBURY: Mrs. W. H. Johnson, BR: early May; WC. NAPOLEON: Fred B. Arps, BR: March 21; WC. NORTH OLMSTED: Mrs. A. Riegelmayer, BR: April; WC. NORWALK: Mrs. Carl Heyman, BR: May-June; WC. OTTAWA: Thomas T. Otto, BR: April; WC. SIDNEY: Roger Protsman, BR: April; WC. SPRINGFIELD: Mrs. Paul E. Hockman, BR: April-June; WC. SWANTON: Mrs. A. A. Beatty, BR: April; WC. TOLEDO: Mahlon P. Leichtamer, BR: March; WC. VAN WERT: Ralph Eck, BR: March and April; WC. WARREN: E. H. Schrader, BR: April and Oct.; WC. WOOSTER: Dr. Henry Loess, BR: April; WC. XENIA: Mrs. William C. Neville, BR: May and June; WC. ZANESVILLE: W. G. Foreman, BR: April and May; WC.

OKLAHOMA

STILLWATER: J. Steve Ownby, Ornamental Horticulturist, Oklahoma State University, Extension Service, BR: April and May; PR: any time the ground is workable; WC. Plant bud union one inch above soil line. Mound soil 8 to 10 inches for winter protection after first hard frost—remove last of March. No fertilizer after August 1.

ANADARKO: Eunice Hollenbeck, BR: Feb. and March; WC. ELGIN: V. Stewart Gwenaniere, BR: Feb. and March; PR: fall; WC. GARBER: Mrs. Earl McFarland, BR: Nov.-March 15; WC.

OREGON

AURORA: Robert L. Ticknor, North Willamette Experiment Station, BR: Nov. to March west of Cascade Mts.; PR: any month. BR: March to April east of Cascade Mts.; PR: March 1 thru June; WC.

ASHLAND: Pearl Dowen, BR: late March, early April; PR: to 1st week in June. Betty Lou Dunlop, BR: Feb.-March; PR: May-June; WC. Ruth Moberly, BR: Feb. CORVALLIS: J. A. Milbrath, BR: Dec.-March. DALLAS: N. John Hansen, BR: Jan.-Feb. GRANTS PASS: Irene Furlong, BR: April-June; PR: April-Sept. KLAMATH FALLS: Mrs. H. M. Munsell, BR: late April; WC. LEBANON: Cecil M. King, BR: Feb. PORTLAND: Mrs. Ben F. Bader, BR: Feb.-Sept.; PR: all year; little WC. ROSEBURG: Dr. I. J. Seitz, BR: Oct.-Nov.; PR: any time; WC. SALEM: Gene Carey, Feb.-March. Ollie Schendel, Nov.-March. WECOMA BEACH: V. R. Ruscoe, Feb.-June.

PENNSYLVANIA

UNIVERSITY PARK: Robert P. Meahl, Pennsylvania Agricultural Experiment Station, BR: April, Oct.; PR: May-June; WC.

ALLENPORT: O. O. Scott, BR: March-April; PR: April. ALLISON PARK: Mrs. W. C. Zahniser, Jr., BR: April; WC. AMBLER: Robert F. Blose, BR: Sept.-Oct.; WC. AUDUBON: Harold R. Crawford, BR: April. BANGOR: O. K. Sorensen, BR: April; WC. BATH: Mrs. D. Artinger, BR: April or Oct. BERWICK: Corola V. Albertson, BR: April; WC. BETHLEHEM: George Gall, BR: April; WC. BLAIRSVILLE: Mrs. H. C. Aldrich, BR: April; WC. BROOKHAVEN, CHESTER: Mrs. A. E. DiCarlo, BR: Nov.; PR: any time; WC. BROOKVILLE: Sarah Allen, BR: April; WC. DRAVOSBURG: Mrs. Velma W. Shoop, BR: Oct.-April; WC. FRANKLIN: S. G. Davis, BR: Sept. and Oct.; WC. EPHRATA: Mrs. Norman W. Keller, BR: March-April; WC. ERIE: Mrs. Anita Gehrlein, BR: April; WC. GILBERTSVILLE: Robert Beldyk, BR: April; WC. GREENSBURG: Mrs. J. M. Bentz, BR: April-May; WC. HARRISBURG: Mrs. J. Hoffer Detweiler, BR: Oct.; WC. KITTANNING: Mrs. Margaret C. Parker, BR: April. LECK HILL: Mrs. Ralph Masser, BR: March and April; WC. LITITZ: Robert W. Etter, BR: April; PR: May; WC. LYKENS: Mrs. Paul P. Shadle, BR: late Oct.; WC. PERKASIE: Mrs. Joseph Lippincott, BR: April-May. PHILADELPHIA: Mrs. Helen Ayen, BR: May-June. L. E. Ingling, BR: March; PR: April; WC. Bernard H. Webb, BR: Oct.; WC. PITTSBURG: Mrs. Dorothy Beisner, BR: Oct. and April; WC. George Cuno, BR: April; WC. Charles Easler, BR: April-Oct.; WC. Howard Keefer, BR: June; PR: May-Aug.; WC. Mrs. J. L. Riddell, BR: April-May. READING: Mrs. John F. Kane, BR: May, WC. SAINT MARYS: A. A. Haberberger, BR: April-May; WC. SCRANTON: Robert E. Dawson, BR: May; WC. SEWICKLEY: Mrs. M. F. Fifer, BR: May; PR: May-Oct.; WC. TARENTUM: Louis Kablusek, BR: Oct.-April; WC. WILLIAMSPORT: John A. Kaiser, BR: April; WILKES-BARRE: Mrs. M. P. Bitler, BR: Oct.-Nov.; WC. YOUNGWOOD: Mrs. Nora Matthews, BR: May; WC.

RHODE ISLAND

KINGSTON: Robinson J. Hindle, Horticulture Dept., University of Rhode Island, BR: early April; PR: most of season; WC. Rhode Island, being a small state, has a fairly uniform climate. We have a shore area where plants will grow and bloom through November. (I have picked a rose at Christmastime at the beach.) We recommend planting roses with the graft union 2 inches below the soil line; winter protection by mounding, wind screens, and rose collars.

BRISTOL: Anthony DiCianni, BR: late Oct., early Nov.; WC. COVENTRY: Mrs. Richard Lamb, BR: April and Oct.; PR: March-Oct.; WC. LINCOLN: Ernest Pollitt, BR: April; WC. PROVIDENCE: Angelo Belmonte, BR: April; PR: April; WC. WAKEFIELD: Mrs. D. W. Hol-

---

BR—Planting time for bare root roses. PR—Planting time for potted roses. WC—Winter care is required. (Whenever WC does not appear, the area does not require winter care.)

gate, BR: May; PR: June; WC. WARWICK: Richard V. Yanco, BR: June and July; PR: Sept. 15-Oct. 10; WC.

PUERTO RICO

RIO PIEDRAS: William Pennock, University of Puerto Rico, BR: any time with irrigation; otherwise avoid dry season between Feb. and April; PR: same as bare roots. Our climate at sea level is slightly too warm for best performance of roses. We therefore have to select varieties best adapted, which include Radiance, Red Radiance, Mrs. Charles Bell, William R. Smith, Mirandy, Crimson Glory and Forty-Niner. Best microclimate at 2,000 feet altitude to the south of the central mountain range where it is not too wet. Worst disease: blackspot. Mildew not a problem except in wet mountain areas.

SOUTH CAROLINA

CLEMSON: F. W. Thode, Assoc. Prof., Department of Horticulture, Clemson University, BR: Dec. to March; PR: any month. Only winter care needed is cutting back long growth in November. Most South Carolina soils are very acid—recommend liming to pH 6.5.

AIKEN: B. C. McLean, BR: March. ANDERSON: Mrs. Jack Ross, BR: Feb.; WC. BOWMAN: Mrs. Henry L. Dukes, Jr., BR: Feb.; PR: any time in spring; WC. GREENVILLE: Arthur Cottingham, Jr., BR: late Jan., early Feb. HARTSVILLE: Mrs. W. F. Burney, Jr., BR: Dec.-Jan.; PR: Feb.-early March; WC. PELZER: R. M. Fennell, BR: Feb.; PR: Nov.-May; WC. SPARTANBURG: Charles Lea, BR: Nov. and March.

SOUTH DAKOTA

BROOKINGS: Ronald M. Peterson, Agricultural Experiment Station, South Dakota State College, BR: May; PR: May-June; WC. Roses are not reliably hardy in South Dakota and in some winters many of them may be killed. Therefore it is advantageous to plant any roses, bare root or potted, as early in the season as possible so that they may be enjoyed during the growing season in which they are planted.

ABERDEEN: J. F. Ehrmann, BR: late April; WC. BERESFORD: Miss Evelyn Soderstrom, BR: late April, early May; PR: May and June; WC. BROOKING: Mrs. Marjorie Whitmore, BR: April-May; WC. FLANDREAU: Mrs. Oliver Larson, BR: May 1; WC. HOT SPRINGS: Mrs. Margaret Wilcox, BR: April; PR: May 15 on; WC. NAPLES: J. C. Kirkeby, BR: May-June; WC. MARTIN: Mrs. C. B. Millar, BR: May; WC.

TENNESSEE

KNOXVILLE: Joseph S. Alexander, University of Tennessee, BR: March-May; PR: March-May, Oct.

ATHENS: Mrs. James F. Cooke, BR: Nov. and March; WC. CLIFTON: T. N. Waters, PR: Dec.-Feb.; PR: March-April. KNOXVILLE: Mrs. Horace H. Binder, BR: March; PR: before

---

BR—Planting time for bare root roses. PR—Planting time for potted roses. WC—Winter care is required. (Whenever WC does not appear, the area does not require winter care.)

June 30; WC. Fred G. Huettel, BR: Feb. LEBANON: William D. Baird, BR: Nov. and March; WC. MEMPHIS: Fred N. Peebles, BR: March. NASHVILLE: Mrs. W. R. Greenfield, BR: March; WC.

TEXAS

TYLER: E. W. Lyle, Plant Pathologist, Texas Rose Research Foundation, BR: Dec.-Jan. for region within 100 miles of coast. Feb.-March for inland area west and north; PR: March through April (but can be done even later); WC: only in far west and north, and then only a couple of inches of soil. The climate and soil vary a great deal from the coast inward and treatment therefore depends on the particular location in the state. From *The Response of Garden Roses*, prepared by A. F. DeWerth of the Texas Agricultural Experiment Station: Most Texas areas, except the Panhandle, have a brief dormant period in late January or during February, which is the most desirable time to plant bare root roses. Container-grown plants can be successfully planted if they are in active growth when transplanted.

Prepare the bed by spading or tilling to a depth of 12 inches. Spread a mixture of 50 percent horticultural grade perlite and 50 percent coarse peat moss over the area to a depth of 4 inches. Mix in thoroughly with existing soil. If experience indicates the possibility of soil-borne diseases, fumigate with a liquid carbamate soil fumigant. Prune roots (or dormant plants) to 12 inches and tops to an outside eye 6 to 8 inches above the bud union. Set bud union at about an inch below soil line. When all plants have been set, water the bed thoroughly. When the surface of the soil shows signs of drying, water the bed with a commercial root-stimulator at the rate recommended. Apply a 2-inch mulch, such as granulated peat moss, cottonseed hulls, ground corncobs, sawdust, sugar cane pulp, ground gin trash, or the like.

In areas where mild winters prevail, remove any dead or broken branches in the spring. Prune back the remainder to 8 to 10 inches from the ground. In colder areas delay pruning until the new buds begin to turn red or danger of killing frost is over. During growing season remove spent flowers, but do not prune plants in any other way except when cutting flowers for indoors.

BEAUMONT: Mrs. B. F. Park, BR: Jan.-April; PR: April-June; WC: on newly planted roses.
BIG SPRING: Mrs. C. L. Marchbanks, BR: Nov.-Feb.; PR: late Sept. thru mid-May; WC.

UTAH

LOGAN: B. Wesenberg, Utah State University, BR: March-May; PR: entire growing season if irrigated properly; WC. Too dry in Utah for fall planting. Much variation from severe climate at higher elevations (considerable winter protection) to fairly mild areas (little winter protection). Fungus diseases no problem.

BOUNTIFUL: Clara Pettey, BR: April; PR: April; WC. KAYSVILLE: Richard C. Hendricksen, BR: May-June; PR: May-July; WC. LOGAN: Mrs. John D. Schultz, BR: mid to late April; PR: June; WC. MAGNA: Mrs. Darwin Petersen, BR: April or May; PR: Sept.; WC. SALT LAKE CITY: Mrs. R. V. Morris, BR: mid-April; WC. Richard H. Parker, BR: May; PR: May.

VERMONT

BURLINGTON: Harrison L. Flint, University of Vermont, BR: April 15-May 15; PR: May and June; WC. Our recommendations on winter protection are subject to change. (Mr. Flint's suggestions for winter protection of hybrid roses in Vermont, printed in full in Chapter 6, "Rose Culture for Special Areas.")

BELLOWS FALLS: Mrs. Lawrence L. Haynam, BR: April; WC. Edward A. Johnson, BR: late May, early June; WC. BURLINGTON: Mrs. Norman R. Greenough, BR: May-early June; PR: May and June; WC. GRAND ISLE: Mrs. Stuart D. Norton, BR: late April; PR: until mid-June; WC. HARDWICK: Mrs. Susan A. Larrabee, BR: April-May; PR: April-July; WC. JERICHO: Mrs. Isabel L. Saccocia, BR: late May-early June; PR: same; WC. MIDDLEBURY: Gordon Bridges, Jr., BR: early May; WC. NEWFANE: Harold W. Whitaker, BR: May; WC. ST. JOHNSBURY: Mrs. W. W. Coomk, BR: late April-early May; WC.

VIRGIN ISLANDS

ST. CROIX: Richard M. Bond, BR: as soon as available in fall; PR: Sept. 15-Dec. 15. We have no cool weather and hence no dormancy for northern varieties. Under best care they only last a year or two. A few of the modern floribundas and more of the very old varieties with a large percentage of south Chinese "blood" last indefinitely, though they are small-flowered and not very attractive. They bloom all the year round and need no rest period. Conditions are uniform throughout the Virgin Islands at least as far as roses are concerned.

VIRGINIA

NORFOLK: Frederic Heutte, Norfolk Botanical Gardens, BR: March; PR: prefer bare root in season: The above applies to the Tidewater Virginia area.

ACCOMAC: Mrs. William K. Wrightson, BR: Feb.-March; ANNANDALE: Mrs. Clinton E. Arnold, BR: Oct.-March; Mrs. William E. Atkins, BR: early March; WC. Marvin Birdsong, BR: late Nov.-March 15; PR: March and April; WC. APPOMATTOX: Orie J. Millner, BR: Nov. BAYSIDE: H. Earl Bennett, BR: Nov. and March or early April; WC. Mrs. P. J. Evans, BR: Oct. BELLAMY: Mrs. George T. Walker, BR: April and May, Oct. and Nov.; WC. BLACKSBURG: Virginia McNeil, BR: March; PR: Feb.; WC. BLUEFIELD: Lillian Hershberger, BR: April-May 15; WC. Mrs. Jack Spraker, BR: March. BUFFALO JUNCTION: Mrs. B. M. Stembridge, PR: Nov. and March or April. CLINCHPORT: Mrs. Ray Russell, BR: March. CULPEPER: Mrs. R. T. Carleson, BR: late March, and April; WC. DRYDEN: Rita Bowling, BR: April; WC. EARLYSVILLE: Mrs. Keith B. Wiley, BR: March-April. EWING: Mrs. Tom B. Fugate, PR: March; WC. FAIRFAX: Mr. and Mrs. C. Ed Alley, BR: April-July; WC. Frank E. Chandler, BR: March and April. Harold O. Jenkins, BR: Oct. or March. FALLS CHURCH: Martha Newman, BR: Nov.-Dec. J. H. Prager, BR: March; WC. Mrs. A. V. Tunison, BR: Nov. and March. FORK UNION: Mrs. Ellis P. Snead, BR: Nov. FREDERICKSBURG: Mrs. Louise B. Hamman, BR: May; WC. HARRISONBURG: Herbert B. Whitmer, Sr., BR: March. ROANOKE: Mrs. C. M. Buck, BR: March; WC. C. H. Lewis, BR: late Nov. or early March.

WASHINGTON

PUYALLUP: Robert A. Wearne, Western Washington Agri. Exp. Station, BR: Western Washington, Nov.-March; Eastern, March-April; PR: the same times plus the growing season; WC: Eastern Yes; Western No. Dormant lime sulphur keeps diseases under control and should be applied January or February. Bi-monthly applications of a fungicide-insecticide combination during the growing season.

CARLSBORG: A. H. Newcomb, BR: Feb. and March. COLFAX: Mrs. Norman H. Kunze, BR: March 15-April 1; WC. HAY: Mrs. Arthur Endsley, BR: April-May; PR: May; WC. OLYMPIA: John H. Vertner, BR: Feb.-March;PR: May-June; WC. PUYALLUP: John M. Jones, BR: Feb.-March; PR: any time. SPOKANE: Firth J. Chew, BR: April-May 1; WC. Victor N.

Runberg, BR: after March 15; WC. TOLEDO: Mrs. Guy E. Brown, BR: March, WC. WENAT-CHEE: Winston E. Brady, PR: March; PR: March-May; WC.

WEST VIRGINIA

MORGANTOWN: Clifford W. Collier, Jr., State Extension Specialist, Landscape Architecture, West Virginia University, BR: March thru mid-April; PR: any time. If forced in greenhouse then only after danger of frost is past; WC. Soil conditions throughout the State are generally suitable for the cultivation of roses. Acid, clay soils predominate except along the Ohio River where sandy soils are often found. All soils may be rendered suitable for rose culture by the addition of lime, organic matter and appropriate fertilizers.

Disease aspects—high humidity of this region makes the control of blackspot an important phase of rose culture.

West Virginia, because of its relatively low latitude, is in a belt of frequent freezes and thaws, which plays an important role in plant survival. Therefore, winter protection of mounding soil around the plants after the ground has frozen generally prevents winter damage.

AURORA: Mrs. Frank Stemple, BR: late April; PR: late May; WC. BECKLEY: Mrs. Augustine Honanski, BR: Nov.-March; WC. CHARLESTON: Robert M. Dixon, BR: April; WC. ELBERT: Mrs. Betty Rae Myers, BR: April-Oct.; WC. SISSONVILLE: James H. Dew, BR: March; PR: no later than May; WC. WHEELING: Mrs. Robert M. Bell, BR: April-May; PR: any time; WC.

WISCONSIN

MADISON: L. M. Berninger, Extension Specialist Commercial Floriculture, Wisconsin Cooperative Extension Service, University of Wisconsin, BR: early to mid-May in southern Wisc., mid to late May in northern Wisc.; PR: mid to late May and early June in northern areas; WC. Homeowners principally concerned with control of blackspot and mildew believe that both problems contribute to the loss of roses during the winter season. Winter protection: it is highly desirable to mulch roses with soil after the first good killing frost and again with marsh hay after the ground freezes. Some of the new "cones" can be used in combination with soil to counteract problems of ice and soil heaving.

ADELL: Mr. and Mrs. John J. Raml, BR: May-June; PR: May-June; WC. APPLETON: Mrs. E. Farrell, BR: May; WC. ARKDALE: Ella Sauer, BR: May; WC. ARPIN: W. Whittingham, BR: April; WC. AURORAVILLE: Mrs. Clifford A. Olsen, BR: May; WC. BELOIT: A. R. Kammerer, BR: May; WC. BROOKFIELD: D. T. Cooper, BR: April; PR: May; WC. Karl Krakow, BR: April-May; WC. CHETEK: Dr. W. H. Woodard, BR: mid-May to early June; WC. CUDAHY: Vanine Pratt, BR: May; WC. ELKHORN: William P. Jacobsen, BR: April-May; WC. FRANKLIN: Lesie M. Munts, Jr., BR: April-May; WC. JANESVILLE: Ralph Honeysett, BR: late May; WC. LACROSSE: Donald Senn, BR: March-April; WC. MADISON: G. P. Schneider, BR: April-May; WC. MANITOWOC: G. J. Napiezinski, BR: April; WC. MARINETTE: N. S. Nelson, BR: May; WC. MARSHFIELD: Mrs. Wayne E. Deming, BR: April; WC. MENASHA: Mrs. Gerard Rasmussen, BR: April-May; WC. MARSHFIELD: Herbert Stoltzman, BR: May; WC. MILTON: Mrs. Velma Hull, BR: April-May; WC. MILWAUKEE: Mrs. Frank Burns, BR: May; PR: early June; WC. Louis Gruska, BR: April; WC. Mrs. R. H. Lambert, BR: May; WC. Mrs. Thomas E. Schneider, BR: spring; WC. H. C. Gumtow, BR: April; PR: May; WC. MONROE: Mrs. Carl Stuckey, BR: spring; WC. RICE LAKE:

BR—Planting time for bare root roses. PR—Planting time for potted roses. WC—Winter care is required. (Whenever WC does not appear, the area does not require winter care.)

W. J. Ustruck, BR: April-May; WC. RIVER FALLS: Dwight Doorak, BR: early May; PR: June; WC. WAUKESHA: Mrs. Warren H. Lubnow, BR: spring; WC.

WYOMING

LARAMIE: Charles W. McAnelly, University of Wyoming, BR: May thru July; PR: June thru Aug., WC. At elevations of 6,000 feet or higher it is not desirable to plant bare root roses before May 20 and potted or canned roses before June 10. Freezing temperatures in early June and late August condition the time of planting at these elevations.

Roses in all areas of the state.should be mulched and covered in some manner to insure survival and satisfactory flower production. This helps prevent dessication and provides protections from extreme cold.

ALADDIN: Mrs. Dean Bailey, BR: April-May; PR: May-June and Sept.; WC. CASPER: Paul L. Clavier, BR: late March: PR: early March; WC. CHEYENNE: C. O. Skjervem, BR: April; WC. LANDER: Mrs. W. Francis Smith, BR: April 20-May 10; WC. ROCK SPRINGS: Raymond J. Albo, BR: April 15-May 15; PR: May 15-30; WC. Mrs. W. E. Smith, BR: April; WC.

INDEX

Khayyam, Omar, 94
King, Dick, 144
Kiosk, *Plate 2*
Knight, Mrs. John W., Jr., 124
Knob, *Plates 43, 44*
Knossos, Palace of, 19

La Quintinie's Herball, 22
Labeling, 80
Ladybirds, 84, 85, 97
Lafe, Mrs. C. W., 123
Language of the rose, 35-36
Larvae, 84
Latoski, Walter, 144
Lavender roses, 22
   photographing, 143-144
Leaching, 95, 97
Leaf mold, 97
Leaf spot, 181, 182
Legends, 31-36
   American, 31
   Chinese, 34
   English, 35
   German, 31
   Greek, 31-32
   Indian, 14, 32
   Jewish, 31
   Middle-Eastern, 35
   Persian, 36
   Turkish, 31
Les Roses, 26
Lewis, C. H., 181
Lice, 83
Lime, 96
Lineage, 110, *Drawing 15*
Linnaeus, 22
Lisanti, Vincent, *Plate XL*
Lists of all known varieties, 103
Loam, 97
Look magazine, 151
Ludwig, Kaiser, 32-34

Macedonia, 20
Maggots, insect, 84
Magnesium, 96
Magnolia, 28
Mailboxes, accessories for, 63
Maine, 191
Malmaison, Chateau of, 26
Manure, 75, 84, 95, 97
Marsh hay, 98
Martial, 21
Marx, Louise, 96-97
Marvin, Don, 144
Mason-Dixon Line, growing south of, 95-96
Medical attributes and uses, 21-22, 131-134
Mendel, Gregor, 26

Mendelian theory, 108
Metal foil wrapping of plants, 97
Mexican chest, *Plate 86*
Miami, Florida, 191
Midas, 20
Mildew, 73, 74, 77, 83, 96, 181, 182
Miller, E. Alvin, 28
Miniatures, 40, 52, 53, 63, 82, *Plates 23, 24*
Minton, Mrs. John W., 125
Miracles, 32-34
Mnesitheus, 131
Modern roses, 26-27, 40
Modern Roses, 103
Mohammed, 31, 35
Moisture, 74, 83
   conservation of, *Plate 50*
   excessive, 95
   retention, 84
Montage, photo, 149
Monticello, 27
Moors, 22
Mounding, 99
Mount Vernon, 27
Mulch paper, 111
Mulches (mulching), 74, 80, 82, 83, 84, 86,
   95, 96, 98, 99, 191-212, *Plates 46-50*
Multiflora, 36, 50, 104, 106, 197
Mumtaz Mahal, 135
Museum of Modern Art sculpture garden,
   Plates 25-28
Mutants, 105

Name(s), 13-14, 80
   of new varieties, 103
   plates, 80
Napoleon, 26
National Council of State Garden Clubs, 122
National flower, bill to designate rose as, 28
Native roses, see Wild roses
Natural History, 21
Nebuchadnezzar, 19
Needlepoint holders, 125, *Plate 65*
   use of in photography, 149, 151-153, 156
Needles, 188
Nematodes, 95
Nero, 21
New England, Northern, 98
New Jersey, 60
New Orleans, 96
New varieties, 171, 183
   developing, 101-114
      cost of, 107
      objectives in, 107
   distinguishing characteristics of, 105
   European, 106-107
   requirements for claiming, 105
   testing, 107, 111, 164